INSIDE SWISS BANKING

The Sudden and Seismic Transformation

Of A Global Financial Brand

Beat J. Guldimann, LLD

Copyright © 2009 by Beat J. Guldimann

All rights reserved. The use of any part of this publication reproduced, transmitted in any form or by any means, electronical, mechanical, photocopying, recording, or otherwise, or stored in a retrieval system, without the prior written consent of the publisher is an infringement of copyright law.

ISBN: 978-0-557-16584-1

Acknowledgments

This book would not have been possible without the many different interactions and the sometimes heated exchanges of opinions I was so privileged to experience with my former colleagues at Swiss Bank Corporation and UBS. I owe a good part of my professional growth, the accumulation of knowledge and the expertise I gained in the field of global private banking to the many lifelong friendships with them.

Thank you to Hilary Carter, Bernard Lette and Paul Duckett for reading the manuscript and for their guidance on the work in progress.

Finally, this book is for my wife Marcella and my children Leslie, Colin and Alan in acknowledgment of their understanding, support and sacrifice on countless weekends and nights spent writing.

iv

Preface

After spending the better part of my professional life directly or indirectly involved in the world of Swiss Banking, I have long felt that the excitement of my work as legal counsel with one of the world's leading institutions had the making of a story worth writing down. Recent events surrounding UBS and the exposure of Swiss private banks to the US judicial system's unwavering zeal for pushing foreign institutions into submission have reignited my desire to provide an insider's view on the mysteries of Swiss Private Banking.

Readers who start reading this book with the hopes of finding juicy details on the dealings of well-known individuals with private banking institutions in Switzerland will be disappointed to find nothing of substance in this book. They should not read on, refrain from buying the book and stick with fiction. The objective of this book is not to share confidential information, it is not a tell-all affair that will make the gnomes in Zurich and many wealthy individuals across the globe tremble. The objective is simply to provide an insider's perspective on how Swiss private banks work, what legal framework guides them and how they navigate through the choppy waters of international law and jurisdictional battles to protect the legitimacy of anyone's desire to keep personal information confidential within the limitations imposed by law.

2009 has proven to be a milestone year for Swiss private banking as the US led an aggressive initiative against UBS as a representative for the Swiss banking sector. The global recession, also started by the United States, led to an increasing appetite of Governments across the OECD to go after citizens that had assets hidden offshore in an effort to limit their exposure to taxation. Governments across the universe were finding their treasuries racking up deficits as taxpayers' money was deployed to stimulate a global economy that had found itself in an irreversible tailspin. In this environment of salvation and sacrifice offshore tax delinquency could no longer be tolerated as just an inconvenient fact of fiscal policy. Paired with an almost incomprehensible level of disregard for global regulation and bank policies demonstrated by some greedy Swiss private bankers, the events of 2008 and 2009 created the backdrop for an unprecedented campaign against Swiss banks and the Swiss financial regulatory system. This book's objective is to explain how the Swiss banking system got to where it was before the summer of 2009 and what the changes of 2009 will likely mean for the future of private banking in Switzerland.

TABLE OF CONTENTS

1	Swiss Banking and Bank Secrecy Explained	1
2	Helvetic Idiosyncrasies	6
3	Keepers of Secrets, Dog Walkers and Concierges	12
4	The Myth of Anonymous Numbered Accounts	21
5	Banking & Swiss Cheese	26
6	Ferdinand Marcos	35
7	Smell Tests and Reputational Pitfalls	54
8	Swiss Banks and the Holocaust	61
9	The Twin Towers	76
10	Swiss Bankers' Code of Due Diligence	83
11	Diamonds and Toothpaste	96
12	Tax Evasion, Fraud and Amnesties	105
13	Swiss Accounts and French Châteaux	115
14	National Sovereignty in a Cross Border Business	123
15	The US Attack on UBS	132
16	The European Union Riding on US Coat Tails	174
17	Levelling the Playing Field in a Global World	186
18	What Happened to the Swiss Brand?	199
	Epilogue	212

List of Abbreviations

AML	Anti-Money Laundering Laws
BRIC	Brazil – Russia – India – China
CDB	Code of Conduct with Regard to the Exercise of Due Diligence of Swiss Banks
DOJ	U.S. Department of Justice
EU	European Union
FATF	Financial Action Task Force
FBI	Federal Bureau of Investigation
FINMA	Finanzmarktaufsicht, formerly SFBC
GDR	German Democratic Republic
GLF	Global Leadership Forum
IRS	U.S. Internal Revenue Service
LGT	Liechtenstein Global Trust
LODH	Lombard Odier Darier Hentsch
NZB	Neue Zuercher Bank
OECD	Organization of Economic Cooperation And Development
PCGG	Presidential Commission on Good Governance
PEP	Politically Exposed Person
SBA	Swiss Bankers' Association
SBC	Swiss Bank Corporation
SFBC	Swiss Federal Banking Commission
SNB	Swiss National Bank
TJN	Tax Justice Network
USA PATRIOT Act	Uniting and Strengthening America by Providing Appropriate Tools Required to Intercept and Obstruct Terrorism Act

CHAPTER ONE

Swiss Banking and Bank Secrecy Explained

Swiss Private Banking and Swiss Bank Secrecy are two terms often used as synonyms. Some say that without the confidentiality created by the stringent rules of bank secrecy as defined in the Swiss Bank Act, there would not be a Private Banking industry in Switzerland. Private Banking and Swiss Bank Secrecy are so much linked in public opinion that legend has it that bank secrecy was invented by the Swiss in the first place. This is not accurate of course as the protection of client confidentiality is inherent to banking in most reliable jurisdictions and the concept of keeping client affairs confidential is probably as old as banking itself. As a matter of fact, the first recognized historical source of banking secrecy may be found in the 1593 statutes of Banco Ambrosiano in Milan, one of the oldest Italian banks which came to doubtful fame centuries later. Ambrosiano collapsed in the 1980s in the aftermath of a $1.4 billion loan scandal involving the Holy See, the head of the Vatican Bank, American-born Cardinal Marcinkus and a secret Masonic society called P2.

On July 17th of 1982 Ambrosiano's President, Roberto Calvi was found on the wrong end of a rope, hanging from London's Blackfriar Bridge with $20,000 in foreign currencies stashed in the pockets of his expensive custom suit. Calvi's death was later ruled a murder and it took until 2007 for a trial to take place. It ended with the acquittal of the five accused. Calvi took the secrets his clients bestowed on him to the grave and we will never know exactly what happened in the secretive triangle of Church, Money and Power. Some say Calvi paid the ultimate price of a banker doing business with the wrong people. Unnatural deaths of Private Bankers, voluntary or not, are a rare occurrence. Unfortunately, the latest turmoil in financial markets produced another pair of such incidents. The month of December 2008 saw two prominent bankers decease: Alex Widmer, Chief Executive of famed and revered Bank Julius Baer died in what appeared to be a suicide; and René-Thierry Magon de la Villehuchet, a French nobleman and financier who invested his and his clients' money with Bernie Madoff saw only one way out of the disgrace that Mr. Madoff's Ponzi scheme put him in.

The point I am trying to make is not that being a senior private banker is inherently dangerous; these are, after all, isolated incidents. What the cases of Calvi, Widmer and Magon show us though is that money carries with it high levels of emotion, especially when there is a lot of it involved. Money is inextricably connected with the fear of

inside swiss banking

investors losing it and their greed to make it grow as much and as fast as possible. Some clients will always keep their cool in front of their banker, no matter how bad the performance is. Others will let their emotions run free and threaten their bankers if things go wrong. Such threats may go well beyond a law suit. While some bankers will always remain professional and focused on delivering the best possible service to their clients, others will fall victim to desperation when confronted with the seemingly insurmountable task of telling their clients the truth about irretrievable losses to a Ponzi scheme. Fear and greed capture investors, their families and their bankers too, though how a person will let fear or greed determine their conduct varies. Private bankers can't escape being caught in the middle as they touch other people's money whenever it moves. Banks and Wealth Managers are used to transfer money from one place to another, to manage deposits made by clients, to extend loans and to invest clients' money in the markets. Clients take their bankers into their fullest confidence for all matters relating to investing and moving their money. In an ever expanding world of compliance and regulation, bankers are expected to know every detail of their clients' financial affairs. While 30 years ago it was not unusual for a wealthy individual to start a long lasting and prosperous relationship with a private bank in Switzerland by simply bringing a briefcase full of cash to a first meeting, those days are long gone. Cash is no longer king in global private banking. Clients will have to deliver proof of a legitimate source of the funds they want to place with their banker. Swiss banks are required to document the details of the client relationship every step of the way, note and track unusual transactions and ask for explanations if there are grounds for suspicion. The new compliance environment requires clients that have traditionally been used to bankers respecting their privilege of discretion to become fully transparent and agree to large files of documents being kept on every financial aspect of their lives. It is no wonder that this raises sensitivities and the expectation that the banks keep the vast amounts of information gathered under the new "Know Your Client" rules (or KYC) confidential and secure from unauthorized access.

For centuries, European monarchs and governments have recognized that the protection of client privacy is critical to ensure a solid banking sector. Without safeguarding client confidentiality there can be no deposit business; without client deposits there can be no lending and without lending there is no economic prosperity. A simplistic view of banking, yes, but centuries ago banking was a pretty straight forward business. This was of course before Wall Street invented collateralized debt obligations and asset backed securities. These simple rules of confidentiality still apply and the expectation of clients for their financial information to be kept safe is magnified by the increase of the amount of information they have to provide to comply with the ever more complex banking regulations around the world. Under the expanding KYC framework banks will gather increasing amounts of confidential information from their clients. Unlike 30 years ago, when confidential data was kept in paper files under lock and key in a senior executive's safe, private banks today use electronic storage devices to manage the ever increasing amounts of data gathered on their clients. Notwithstanding the best IT security frameworks this data is exposed to an increased risk of unauthorized access and uncontrollable exposure. Not too long ago, these risks became a reality as a disgruntled IT specialist at a Liechtenstein-based bank hacked into the IT system, created a list of client names and account numbers and sold it to the German Intelligence Service. This breach of security has created the biggest raid on German clients accused of tax evasion in history and led to prominent members of the German business community having to resign their positions and disappear into the sunset, among them the head of the German postal service. Arguably the Liechtenstein evidence was obtained illegally; the IT specialist broke Liechtenstein law and was allegedly paid by the German Intelligence Service to do so. This would of course ban the use of the evidence under any rule of law. However, the damage to the clients is done regardless; their confidentiality has been breached and authorities have illegally gained access to their information.

CHAPTER TWO

Helvetic Idiosyncrasies

As we have learned in the previous chapter, bank secrecy is no more a Swiss invention than are watches. Yet both are seen as defining features of Helvetic identity. We are not going to explore the merits of what the Swiss have done in the watch industry even though this might be an interesting journey on its own. Let's stay focused on the world of private banking and find some answers to the question: What makes Swiss bank secrecy so different from confidentiality rules in other countries?

The Swiss have long recognized that the personal right to privacy and freedom includes the right to protect financial information. The Swiss Federal Court has ruled to that effect consistently since its establishment in 1874. When Switzerland enacted a Bank Act in 1934, its Article 47 contained criminal sanctions against violations of banking secrecy provisions. Individuals with access to confidential banking information face the risk of not only stiff fines but also prison time if they chose to make such information available to third parties. This is one of the key differentiators of the Swiss rules compared to those of other nations. To understand why the Swiss reinforced the privacy and confidentiality of financial information with criminal sanctions, we need to look at the historic context in which the provisions of the Bank Act were conceived. A year earlier, in 1933, Adolf Hitler became Chancellor in Germany. The Nazis soon enacted the "Economic Treason Act" which was primarily aimed at justifying the expropriation of assets held by German Jews. This Act introduced a requirement for banks to disclose financial information to the Government. Client relationships became transparent to the Nazis and the Economic Treason Act created free access to the assets of anyone in their crosshairs. It should not surprise anyone that this new law caused a heavy outflow of assets from German banks, chiefly to neighbouring Switzerland which at this point already was known as a safe haven with a strong tradition of respecting client privacy. The Nazi Regime in Berlin of course was not known for restraint and reason which would later be proven as the Second World War broke out and the Holocaust took its horrific course.

The brave legislators that drafted the Swiss Bank Act in 1934 understood two things: firstly the Gestapo would not be restrained from crossing the border into Switzerland in an effort to try to intimidate Swiss bankers and convince them of the benefits of giving up financial records; and secondly there was a risk that some Swiss citizens would not only sympathize with the Nazis but actively cooperate with the Gestapo, not so much out of intimidation but because they agreed with the Nazis ideologically. Anti-Semitism was not unique to Germany but a phenomenon spread across Europe, including Switzerland. Thus criminal sanctions were introduced to raise the stakes for anyone that remotely considered breaking secrecy laws. The maximum sentence of six months imprisonment may not serve as effective a deterrent if looked at in isolation. In combination with the likelihood, however, that a convicted felon would not find employment with any bank once they served their sentence, a rather strong incentive had been created for bankers to stay within the boundaries of the law.

Three years later, in 1937, the Swiss Federal Criminal Code came into effect and with it a criminal offence pertaining to economic espionage for foreign individuals, entities or governments. Making banking information available to foreign entities such as the Gestapo became punishable not only under the Bank Act but also under Article 273 of the Criminal Code, violations of which would be sanctioned with imprisonment up to 3 years, in severe cases up to 20 years.

This combination of the contractual obligation of a banker to keep information on their clients confidential with the criminal sanctions imposed by the Bank Act and the Criminal Code is largely what makes the Swiss regime of

inside swiss banking

banking secrecy unique. Not only can bankers be sued by their clients in the civil court system for damages caused by the unauthorized release of their information, they will also be prosecuted under the criminal justice system. Furthermore, a banker convicted of violating banking secrecy rules will almost certainly lose their employment and will be banned from future employment in the industry. Under the framework of Swiss law and regulations and the practice of the Swiss Bankers Association as well as the Federal Financial Regulatory Authority (FINMA) the price for someone considering keeping a loose lip with regards to all the confidential information bestowed on them is one of the highest around the world, arguably topped only by Singapore.

Of course there are boundaries in which bank secrecy rules offer protection. Article 47 of the Bank Act was never designed to protect illegitimate interests. It will be set aside whenever there is an inquiry by a judicial authority such as a prosecutor or a civil court residing in Switzerland. Contrary to what can be read in spy novels and other works of literary fiction, the Swiss private banking framework has never been designed to attract, harbour or tolerate criminals of any shade. We will explore later on how the financial regulation has adapted over the years to counter this misconception and to force financial institutions to adopt due diligence and KYC rules. Today, Switzerland has one of the toughest due diligence frameworks in the world which is used as point of reference for many other jurisdictions.

As some of the leading Swiss private banks expanded their business scope internationally, bank secrecy issues increased in complexity. The Swiss laws and regulations only apply to Swiss territory and as Swiss banks became more active in their business with foreign clients they exposed themselves to the reach of foreign authorities. Their interest in gaining access to confidential banking information pertaining to their citizens often creates a conflict with Swiss secrecy rules. Confidential banking information kept in Switzerland can only be released to a Swiss judicial authority based on a Swiss court order. This is a concept anchored in the principle of national sovereignty which has been established for centuries. However, the globalization of financial services spurred the necessity of increased global cooperation of governments facilitating the exchange of information across borders. In reply to this demand Switzerland has entered into a series of international treaties with all major financial jurisdictions that govern the exchange of information under a common legal assistance protocol. In order for legal assistance to occur there needs to be full reciprocity between the treaty nations as well as dual incrimination of the acts underlying the request for legal assistance. The prerequisite of dual incrimination regularly comes into play in tax related legal assistance cases. Unlike most other countries Switzerland

inside swiss banking

makes a distinction between two degrees of tax infractions; tax evasion for which no criminal sanctions apply and tax fraud which is punishable under the criminal code. As a result of this distinction in Swiss tax law legal assistance to foreign tax authorities or prosecutors will only be available in cases of tax fraud. This in turn results in Swiss bank secrecy rules protecting clients who are evading taxes in their home country. This has long been a thorn in the side of Switzerland's European neighbours but also, and most importantly the United States. The most recent and highly publicised battle between the US and UBS brought this legal dispute to a whole new level. We will explore this story in much more detail later on, including how the Swiss Government recently responded to mounting international pressure to abolish the distinction of tax evasion and tax fraud when dealing with foreign customers.

11

CHAPTER THREE

Keepers of Secrets, Dog Walkers and Concierges

The proverbial Swiss private banker is no doubt seen as a person clients will turn to as a keeper of secrets. The tradition of maintaining and upholding client confidentiality is engrained in the role of a Swiss private banker and the secrecy and privacy framework that has been created in Swiss banking laws supports the bankers in this role. Wealthy families around the globe have sought the confidentiality of Swiss banks to conduct their financial affairs for decades if not centuries due to the unequivocal reputation that Switzerland has created over time for being one of the safest places on the planet to have money on deposit. It became a natural expectation for wealthy individuals and families that the business they conduct with a bank in Geneva or Zurich will not be discussed outside the four walls of the institution under any circumstance. The discretion of a Swiss banker is hard to mimic or exceed and this has led to clients using their bankers as repositories of information that reaches well beyond the simple monetary aspects of their banking relationship.

inside swiss banking

Take Ludovico Montegrosso, an Italian count invented for illustrative purposes whose family traces back into the 13th Century and who is now the controlling shareholder of a flourishing industrial conglomerate in Italy with business around the globe. Ludovico and his family have been clients of Dupont & Cie, Banquiers in Geneva for generations. Yves Dupont is a fifth generation partner at the firm and personally looks after the Montegrosso accounts. This is not just a business relationship in which banking transactions, investments and loans get negotiated; it is a personal friendship that has lasted for generations and where mutual trust has been built over decades between the two families: the Montegrosso family as clients and the Dupont family as trusted bankers. As a result Dupont & Cie is much more than just a bank to the Montegrosso family. Ludovico will have shared a host of confidential information pertaining to his family with Yves and Yves will have been asked for and offered advice on a wide range of issues well beyond the pure business of banking. Yves helped Ludovico find a private school for his children in the Swiss Alps where they have enjoyed adolescence in seclusion away from the public scrutiny their family is exposed to in Italy. Dupont pays the school fees and Yves' personal assistant deals with any issues that may occur between the school and the Montegrosso children on a confidential basis. Yves also arranges for the management of the various properties that Ludovico and his family own

13

outside of Italy: a chalet in Zermatt, an oceanfront condo in Barbados and a couple of flats in London and New York. If these properties come with dogs, Dupont will make sure they have been walked twice a day. Yves also knows about Ludovico's various mistresses and manages the money that the latter has set aside from the family fortune to facilitate their lifestyle and ensure their discretion. Obviously, Yves will know better than to discuss these accounts when meeting with Ludovico and his wife Adriana four times a year. Discretion also applies within the relationship. When Adriana raised suspicion as to Ludovico's extra-marital conduct a few years ago, she placed a confidential call to Yves to enquire about a possibly existing account that her husband might have set up for a woman she had found out about through the services of a private investigator. Yves lips remained sealed. Bank secrecy precluded him from discussing other people's business with anyone, including family members. Adriana understood and never bothered to involve Yves in this regard after this first attempt. As much as she hated the fact that she could not get anything out of Yves, it made her comfortable that the Montegrosso's business was in good hands. Her marriage with Ludovico may be in trouble but this is none of Dupont's concern.

Ludovico and Adriana may not be the happiest couple but they share a concern about their three children getting access to vast amounts of money at an early age should something happen to them. This concern has been

inside swiss banking

taken care of by way of a family foundation. All of the Montegrosso fortune held at Dupont & Cie has been transferred to the foundation of which Yves and one of his partners are the directors in an effort to remove direct control over the assets from the family. This will allow for the family fortune to remain intact across generations and to manage the childrens' access to the money outside of the parents' estate. In order to increase the children's understanding of financial affairs at an early stage, Dupont & Cie offers them summer jobs at the bank and invites them to investment seminars that Dupont puts together from time to time for young members of wealthy families.

The Montegrosso's are known for their love of the arts and for the impressive collection of master paintings that is on display in the Museo d'Arte Montegrosso on the family estate outside of Modena. Ludovico's father Giorgio had started the museum and opened a part of the family estate to the public a couple of decades ago. When Giorgio passed away, the Museo d'Arte was transferred into a public foundation according to his will. The Fondazione Giorgio Montegrosso is a non-profit organization run by a board of directors appointed equally by the State of Italy and the Montegrosso family. Yves is of course one of the directors nominated by the family. As per Giorgio's will, the family is under an obligation to continue supporting the museum through donations of significant works of art. A fund worth several millions of Euros has been set apart under Giorgio's

15

will to that effect. Dupont & Cie manages the fund and represents the family in dealings with Sotheby's and other auction houses in order to ensure confidentiality of any purchases that are being made. After all, the Montegrossos are well known as patrons of the arts and will not bid for a Picasso or Modigliani in person. Since Dupont & Cie has a few clients just like the Montegrosso family, they are known in auction circles as representing various clients with a high demand for discretion. Purchases made by them won't be traced back to their clients unless the clients will allow it after the fact. This helps keep purchase prices low and confidentiality high.

These examples illustrate how private banking Swiss style has embraced the concept of what is known as "Family Office" in North America long before the use of family office services became fashionable among the wealthy from Palm Beach to Palm Springs and from Martha's Vineyard to Seattle. In recent months the raison d'être of Swiss private banking has been portrayed in the media as principally resting on its ability to harbour tax cheats from across the globe. The prominence of the United States attacks against UBS has created havoc not only at this firm but across the Swiss private banking industry and the Swiss government. But as the example of the fictitious Montegrosso family demonstrates, the proverbial confidentiality offered by private bankers in Geneva or Zurich goes much further. To reduce the value of a private banking relationship in Switzerland to that of providing shelter for illegitimate tax purposes is a crass misrepresentation of reality. This is not to say that shelter from international prosecution in tax evasion matters may indeed be a significant factor for some wealthy individuals when choosing a Swiss bank as home for their assets. However, Swiss private banks have much more to offer. Theirs is a centuries-old culture of service to clients and of building long-lasting relationships based on trust and mutual respect as well as a tradition of capital protection and asset diversification. True private banks are much more akin to multi-family offices looking after a variety of issues of concern to wealthy families including generational transfers, philanthropic activity and protection of assets from the ubiquitous threat of unwarranted litigation.

One does not have to be a member of Italian aristocracy to understand the value of a banker's discretion. The culture of keeping client information confidential is beneficial to anyone that puts a high value on financial privacy. It applies to the Latin American client that has an issue with the level of corruption and the lack of confidentiality at domestic banks, not to mention concerns about the political stability in their home country. The security and confidentiality offered by Swiss banks serves as a good solution to keep some rainy day money in a safe place. It also applies to the wealthy Canadian family that has formed a charitable foundation to support humanitarian projects in Africa. The increased confidentiality of locating the foundation offshore sits well with their desire to keep the family's philanthropic initiative outside of the public eye. In addition it allowed them to pool their interest in African affairs with other like-minded families outside of Canada who are supporting the Swiss foundation with major contributions. And lastly, the confidentiality offered by a banker in Basel serves the purpose of a German entrepreneur that is engaged in a legal dispute with a former business partner. Keeping all of his assets with the small regional savings bank in the Black Forest exposes him to the loose lips of a branch manager that is known for indiscretions when having a few drinks at the local watering hole. Moving some of his money across the border eliminates the risk that his personal balance sheet is made available to his former partner outside of court proceedings. Neither of the clients in these three examples chose a Swiss bank to make money disappear from the tax man. They did so in a legitimate effort to protect their wealth from a wide range of potential threats. Nobody will argue that those that have accumulated wealth are entitled to protect it by whatever legal means they deem appropriate. Swiss banking confidentiality is designed to cover the many areas of legitimate interest of wealthy families around the globe. Its purpose is not to assist clients in hiding assets gained from unlawful activities. This is not to say that there are no bankers who would not cross the line and unfortunately

inside swiss banking

there are plenty of examples where bankers have in fact actively assisted illegitimate clients in their unlawful conduct of business. However, this is not an indication that the banking industry or the private banking business models are broken, as some voices would have it. What it indicates is simply that individuals will sometimes decide to disregard rules and regulations in order to further their personal benefit. Greed for higher financial rewards or fear of not achieving performance goals may be a factor playing into these decisions. Some financial institution may be better than others in enforcing compliance with governance and taking measures against management and staff if a problem is detected. At the end of every violation of business policies or regulations and of every transgression of the law we will always find an individual or a group of people. Rarely will these transgressions be systemic in nature, be it for a corporation or even a whole industry. Governance taken seriously requires banks to make sure that policies and ethical standards are put in place and vigorously enforced so that all employees, from the teller to senior private bankers, understand what kind of behaviour is expected and what types of actions will not be tolerated. To this end the Swiss Bankers Association (SBA) has established a stringent set of rules in its Code of Conduct with Regard to the Exercise of Due Diligence (CDB) which have to be followed by all signatory banks and compliance with which is controlled and enforced vigorously by the

19

SBA. We will examine the CDB in more detail later on in this book.

CHAPTER FOUR

The Myth of Anonymous Numbered Accounts

It was a foggy day in Zurich as Justin Lorne woke up after a long journey from the Irkutsk oil fields, the scene of his last assignment, to the shores of Lake Zurich. He had a good nights' sleep at Savoy en Ville, his favourite hotel just off the famed Bahnhofstrasse where he was known as Mr. Smith from Boston. Rudolph Hugentobler, the senior vice president of private banking at Limmat Bank International AG has been expecting Mr. Smith for a visit at his bank. As usual Justin Lorne aka Mr. Smith would withdraw a hundred thousand Swiss francs in cash from his numbered account, providing Hugentobler with the code word he had chosen 12 years ago when he deposited 19 million US dollars in cash: the word "Alphorn" would suffice for Lorne to get his business done. Nobody had to know who he was or where the money came from that he now used to survive as the Atlantic Intelligence Agency had dropped him from its ranks in the aftermath of the unfortunate events in Siberia a week ago.

The above reads like the beginning to a spy novel and it could be something that Tom Clancy or Robert

Ludlum wrote. The stuff of a novel, the story about Justin Lorne and Rudolf Hugentobler would most certainly not play out this way in real life. Just like the character of Justin Lorne, the existence of anonymous numbered accounts with Swiss banks is a pure work of fiction. The Swiss have actually introduced far ranging rules on client identification and requirements to ascertain the legitimate background of the money deposited with banks long before the international community and international organizations such as the Financial Action Task Force (FATF) have latched on to the concept that bankers need to know in any instance who they are dealing with. Nobody can open a bank account in Switzerland without disclosing their identity and providing evidence on the source of funds. This was not always the case though, and hence the legend of anonymous accounts has some basis in history. Up until the early 1990s, Swiss courts had ruled that the client-attorney privilege of lawyers and accountants would extend to financial transactions that members of these two professions carried out on behalf of their clients. As a result, a lawyer or accountant did not have to disclose the identity of their clients as long as they declared on a specific form established as part of the CDB that they had taken appropriate steps to identify the client and that to the best of their knowledge and belief the funds placed with the bank were not connected to illegal activities. The banks were required by case law and bank regulations to rely on the accuracy of statements made by lawyers or accountants and the auditing of the accuracy of the declarations made to the banks was left to the professional organizations such as the respective bar associations. This practice is no longer in place; the client-attorney privilege can no longer be invoked by lawyers and likewise accountants can no longer invoke their professional privilege when dealing with banks.

The requirement of the bank to know the identity of the client extends beyond the account holder. If an account is opened by someone acting in trust for a third party, that third party needs to be identified as well. In case of accounts held by trustees, beneficiaries and/or protectors will have to be named and identified. For accounts held in the name of nominee companies or similar holding vehicles, not only the directors of said company need to be identified but also the individuals carrying a direct or beneficial interest in the shares.

All these requirements apply regardless of whether the account is opened under a personal or corporate name or simply as a numbered account. While anonymous banking relationships can only be found in novels and other works of fiction, numbered accounts do exist. So one might ask what the benefit of identifying oneself as client 38562 is if the bank knows that 38562 stands for Justin Lorne, to take the example of our fictitious secret agent. The answer lies in the heightened confidentiality that Justin Lorne enjoys when dealing with Limmat Bank International AG. He does not have to announce himself by name and except the senior bankers dealing with his account and the management supervising them, nobody in the bank will know who 38562 is. The bank will have done all the required paperwork on Mr. Lorne; a passport copy will be on file together with his last residential address. He will have signed a series of documents with his name, including a declaration that he is the "beneficial owner" of the funds held at the bank. His banking activities will be screened by the bank's compliance department for any unusual transactions that might raise suspicion of potential money laundering activities. However, for day-to-day business with the bank, Justin Lorne will simply be known as client 38562. The bank's mainframe systems will identify the holder of account number 38562 as 38562 and the staff executing transactions for this account will have no idea for whom a bank transfer has been made or received, a series of shares are being purchased or sold. A numbered account can be operated in the normal course of business without the necessity to provide a name. In the bank's beneficial owner database however, Justin Lorne will be found as the person beneficially interested in account 38562. His name will be linked to all activities on this account and in case of judicial inquiries or an internal investigation under federal money laundering regulations the bank will reveal his identity to the authorities under the established processes

inside swiss banking

and protocols, regardless of whether Justin's account was held in his own name, under a company name or simply identified by its number.

CHAPTER FIVE

Banking and Swiss Cheese

The international community loves Swiss stereotypes. The Swiss are always on time; the railroad system's punctuality is proverbial. The Swiss are famous for expensive watches and brands like Rolex and Omega have become synonymous for Swiss quality around the world. The Swiss are secretive about their banking business; we have explored this at length already. Only the Belgians will contest Swiss supremacy when it comes to the art of chocolate. And last but not least the words Swiss and Cheese are an inextricably linked pair. If you were to add the sound of cow bells ringing on a pristine Alpine pasture with someone tooting harmonies into an Alphorn, the picture would be so idyllic you could use it in a 'Ricola' commercial. The Swiss are proud of their cheese making achievements and the many different types of cheese made in the mostly artisanal 'fromageries' around the country but the most famous of them all is one that is produced industrially not only in Switzerland but copied around the world. It is known as 'Emmental' which is the name of the

inside swiss banking

valley where its original is made and it is famous not so much for its taste but because no other cheese comes with bigger holes. It is so famous in fact that around the world it is simply referred to as 'Swiss'. And because of its holes it became the perfect analogy to describe the many limitations of bank secrecy.

As discussed in earlier parts of this book, bank secrecy was never designed to provide absolute protection of client data, financial records and the like. Bank clients acting outside the confines of the law could never rely on Swiss banks keeping their financial affairs confidential from judicial or other government authorities that were going after them. The protection of client confidentiality will generally be set aside if a client's interest to keep things out of reach of the authorities is deemed an illegitimate use of secrecy rules to protect unlawful actions. Of course this is a simplified generalization of the concept and legions of lawyers have made it their business to protect their clients' interests in matters regarding their banking relationship in Switzerland. Whenever disclosure requests are made of a bank they will be challenged, court orders affirming the request will be appealed and invariably attempts will be made to accuse bank managers and executives of violating Section 47 of the Swiss Bank Act, not to mention the civil suits that will ensue seeking compensatory damages from everybody involved.

27

The limitation of the reach of bank secrecy rules, however, is part of the concept itself. Nobody has poked holes in the system of bank secrecy. The principle remains unchanged as one of safeguarding the legitimate interest of a bank client for their privacy and confidentiality to be protected from unauthorized intrusion. Only legitimate interest in confidentiality is protected; the secrecy rules have neither been designed nor intended to provide a safe haven for crooks and criminals and the very integrity of the bank secrecy framework depends on it being protected against abuse. Comparing how bank secrecy has evolved over the past decades with Swiss cheese is therefore amusing but inadequate. But just as the process of fermentation causes the holes in the Emmental cheese to build, domestic and international laws under which Swiss financial institutions operate have been evolving over decades and will continue to do so over time. The language of the section in the Swiss Bank Act dealing with the confidentiality of client information has not changed since it has first been written into law. What has changed is the environment in which financial institutions, their executives and employees as well as their clients operate. Let's use the example of insider trading. Ever since the first trade was made on an organized stock market individuals making these trades have been exploiting confidential knowledge for their own benefit. In the words of Gordon Gecko, the archetype of an aggressive trader in the movie 'Wall Street': 'Greed is good' became

inside swiss banking

the mantra of Wall Street in the Seventies and Eighties. Greed became a major driver for traders of all backgrounds, skill and education levels. He who had the best inside track into what was coming down the pipe in a traded company had the advantage of making a trade before anybody else could, dumping a stock before damaging news became public or buying before a new billion dollar deal was announced. These were the Gold Rush days of Wall Street and other major exchanges around the world. Careers could be made in a single trade and the glory belonged to those who had the best information and took the biggest bets based on it. The 'Masters of the Universe', as Tom Wolfe called them in his novel 'The Bonfire of the Vanities', abused inside information they obtained in confidence with impunity until the law caught up with them in an effort to level the playing field in the market between those participants that happened to have the inside track and those who didn't. In these glory days of trading on inside knowledge nobody would have imagined that one day the Gordon Geckos of the world would be prosecuted for their acts. But the concepts of what was considered ethical behaviour in the financial markets changed and so did the law. Insider trading in which confidential, non-public information on a listed company was being abused for a trader's personal benefit became a criminal offence. As many other nations have done under the leadership of the United States well before it, Switzerland enacted changes to its Criminal Code and introduced insider trading as a new criminal offence in 1988. What used to be perfectly acceptable behaviour on the trading floor became a criminal activity. Bank clients who used to be able to place trading orders with their bankers or brokers with impunity, even if they had inside knowledge, all of a sudden faced the risk of prosecution as well as the risk of their bank reporting them to the judicial authorities. Not a single syllable was changed in the bank secrecy language of section 47 of the Bank Act, yet the protection of client confidentiality under the law had become significantly narrower. What is important to note though is that it was a change in the Criminal Codes across the industrialized world with functioning financial markets that prompted the change, not a revision of the Swiss Bank Act. Nobody punched additional holes in the Swiss cheese; rather, an evolution occurred in our collective societal understanding of what types of behaviour are acceptable and where the line is drawn to determine what actions shall henceforth be treated as criminal activity.

The Swiss Criminal Code was expanded in 1990 with the introduction of another set of new criminal offences that became a game changer for the financial services industry. Alongside other major jurisdictions and in line with guidelines established by international organisations such as the OECD's Financial Action Task Force (FATF), Switzerland issued a criminal tariff on persons engaged in activities that were designed to hide or dissimulate the

inside swiss banking

source of funds connected to criminal offences. These actions are commonly referred to as money laundering. Making them a criminal offence was a declaration of intent to Organized Crime that the Swiss financial services system was no longer available to them in carrying out their banking and investment business. To enhance the practicability of the new money laundering provisions in the Criminal Code, a specific due diligence requirement was introduced in lock-step that made it mandatory for any firm or individual engaged in the financial services sector to ensure that the identity of the person or persons beneficially interested in the funds deposited with them had been ascertained with reasonable prudence. Failure to do so is now a criminal offence in Switzerland. In addition, the new provisions on due diligence in financial matters now include the specific right of banks, investment managers and anybody else professionally involved in financial affairs of clients to report such clients to domestic criminal authorities if they are suspected of engaging in money laundering activities. Those who like the analogy to Swiss cheese will once again find an example of hole punching but just as was the case with the insider trading act of 1988, not a single change has been made to the secrecy provisions in the Bank Act. The introduction of the criminal offences surrounding money laundering are just another example of how the criminal code evolves to catch up with reality and as a result of these new rules it just became a lot harder for

31

criminal elements of all sorts to abuse the Swiss financial sector for their financial objectives.

Most criminal activity has a touch point with money. Following the money trail is often the most rewarding course of action for prosecutors to capture perpetrators and put them behind bars. Criminals, by definition, like cash because it makes tracing their financial conduct more difficult. However, most of them eventually have to find a financial institution somewhere in the world to deposit the fruits of their activities. Bankers around the world can't escape the risk of becoming involved with criminal organisations or individuals but the legal and regulatory framework can raise the stakes by making it painfully complicated to deal with the financial services sector under their jurisdiction, hoping that this will drive as many undesirable clients as possible to take their business elsewhere. What the Swiss legislators have done in 1988 and 1990 is exactly that; they signalled to the world of international crime that Switzerland does not want their business and to some degree they have put the onus on the banking system to execute this newly evolved policy. Some may find that the series of new criminal rules have punched holes in the secrecy framework that had been built in the 1930s. In my view the tough stance on financial crime strengthened the integrity of the framework as it reduced the risk of abuse by criminals and criminal organisations.

inside swiss banking

As we will explore later on a similar evolution is currently underway in tax matters that will no doubt result in significant changes in the way Swiss bank secrecy protection is viewed by the international community and by foreign clients that have deposited part of their assets with Swiss banks in the hopes of being able to hide their existence from their home country's tax authorities. Switzerland has long been under mounting pressure from the European Union and the United States to grant legal assistance to their tax authorities, not only in cases of fraud, but also in cases of tax evasion. The Swiss Government has very recently signalled that they are prepared to make respective changes to tax treaties with both the U.S. and the E.U. To some, this will look like surrendering the very essence of Swiss secrecy in banking matters but this view reduces the value of the confidentiality rules to providing shelter to individuals and corporations trying to hide assets from their government's reach. As we have seen in the case of the imaginary Montegrosso family, there is much more to the confidentiality engrained in the Swiss private banking tradition. The value proposition of a Swiss private bank clearly is much deeper than providing shelter from foreign tax authorities. Swiss banks and bank secrecy rules will survive the impending changes to the international legal assistance framework as they continue to evolve in the context of continued change in the legal environment in which they operate. Adaptation to new rules and regulations is a key requirement today just as it was in 1990 and 1988 and during any time of significant change before that.

CHAPTER SIX

Ferdinand Marcos

If there was a contest for the most infamous political figure of the 20th Century, Ferdinand Marcos (1917-1989) would have an excellent shot at winning it. The former leader of the Philippines for 21 years (1966 to 1986) shaped the common definition of a dictator and has become the incarnation of all evil we associate with how dictators exercise power: bribery, elimination of competitors by assassination, diverting of foreign aid for personal benefit, expansion of cronyism, ultimate control over political and economical power in the nation under his grip; the list goes on. He was one of the strong men of South East Asia and a friend of the U.S. during the Vietnam War and in the fight against the spread of Communism. Even though a ruthless dictator, he was a person the world would do business with as a statesman and an individual alike. Among the many companies engaged with the Marcos family were Swiss banks, most notably Swiss Bank Corporation and Credit Suisse where Marcos had deposited significant amounts of money for safe keeping. After all, the Swiss had a reputation of confidentiality and of respecting their most important clients' need for privacy. These were the Sixties and Seventies, a time long before too many questions were asked when someone wished to open a bank account. These were the times before FATF rules and the global fight against corruption, money laundering and organized crime. These were times in which Ferdinand and Imelda Marcos would be greeted with a red carpet wherever they went, including state visits to Bern, London, Hong Kong or Washington. In the Sixties and Seventies it was not unusual for people in political power to personally bank in a safe place. Maybe their personal fortunes did not pass the smell test in all regards but at the time there was no regulation that prohibited banks from dealing with questionable dictators or their families. As long as Ferdinand Marcos or any of his peers in other developing countries were in power, no questions had to be asked about the source of wealth. The world was not sensitive to the ethical dilemmas that corruption created or at least these sensitivities were much less important than they are today. Bankers thought nothing of dealing with powerful politicians; in fact there was just no way that any bank would refuse to deal with them. After all these were well connected and in some instances even well respected world leaders with direct access to the Presidents of the United States or France, the Prime Minister of the United Kingdom and the Government in Switzerland. So, as long as Ferdinand

inside swiss banking

Marcos was in power, it was business as usual for banks in different financial centres including Switzerland to look after his and Imelda's money and to give them the VIP treatment that their status asked for.

Things changed dramatically in 1986 when Ferdinand Marcos was ousted into exile after friends like the U.S. turned to foes in the aftermath of a rigged election that eventually brought Corazon Aquino to power in the Philippines. Marcos, his family and the inner circle of his associates settled in Hawaii in the hopes of finding a soft landing from public power and continue their lives as private citizens while enjoying the benefit of wealth accumulated in banks in the U.S. and elsewhere. Unfortunately for them, retirement from public office did not turn out quite this way. The story surrounding the vast accumulation of wealth that Ferdinand Marcos had orchestrated during his 20 years in power became a veritable saga of multiple claimants battling in courts around the globe for access to the Marcos assets. Two Swiss banks holding the bulk of the assets that had been funnelled into Switzerland over the years found themselves right in the middle of it. While the banks' relationship with the Marcoses dates back to the sixties and seventies, the problems with the accounts started when Ferdinand Marcos was forced from power into exile in 1986.

37

In an unprecedented move only one month after Marcos fled to Hawaii, the Swiss Federal Council issued an executive order freezing all assets held in Switzerland for Marcos, his extended family and/or associated cronies. This 1986 freeze order was new territory in that it was not issued by a judicial body but directly by the Swiss executive branch. There was no formal request for legal assistance either as no criminal case had obviously been established yet against Marcos and his many cronies in the first days of the new administration in the Philippines. So why did the Swiss Federal Government resort to emergency powers granted to the executive branch in the Swiss Constitution to prevent access to the Marcos assets? Two things happened: When the new administration in Manila swept through the Presidential Palace in Malacanang, they found a series of documents relating to bank accounts held by Marcos and his associates in Switzerland. The so-called "Malacanang Documents" were later used to support a request for legal assistance that the Aquino government submitted to the Swiss authorities. Meanwhile, as the Aquino administration was preparing a case against Marcos for corruption, bribery, graft and other criminal acts, a Filipino national acting on a power of attorney attempted to access assets deposited by Marcos with one of the Swiss banks. Given the political noise around Marcos' fall from grace and power, this bank thought it prudent not to allow the requested transfer of assets to neighbouring Austria as intended by Marcos'

inside swiss banking

attorney but instead to report the attempted transfer to the Swiss authorities.

With a legal assistance request from Manila imminent and in light of the global outrage against Marcos and the abuse of Presidential power he was associated with, the Swiss Federal Council took the extraordinary measure of freezing all Marcos assets in Switzerland to protect vital Swiss national interest. Since none of the technical requirements had been met for a judicial freeze order under the mutual legal assistance framework that Switzerland had established only five years earlier, an executive order was the only tool available to halt any transfers of Marcos assets out of the jurisdiction. There was just no way that the Swiss Government would stand idly by as one of the most infamous dictators the world had ever known was trying to access the ill gotten wealth he stole from his own people. Sitting on the sidelines was not one of the available avenues. One can only imagine the public's reaction around the globe if it had turned out that the government knew that toxic Marcos assets had been moved out of the country moments before the Aquino administration requested their sequestration. Switzerland would have been portrayed in the global media as a nation that facilitates graft and corruption. Swift action with regards to what was rapidly becoming a global scandal was indeed the only option if Switzerland was to maintain its reputation as a functioning financial centre that respects its obligations towards the

39

international community. Too much was at stake. Switzerland, a small country whose economy relies heavily on export and leveraging international connections to produce a GDP that its population of some 7 million could not possibly reach on its own, could not risk global isolation as a result of a few of its banks doing business with a dictator that had fallen from grace.

The Marcos family was thus denied access to the assets sitting with Swiss Banks even though no proof had been delivered that they were guilty of any criminal acts. De facto this meant that the presumption of innocence until proven guilty was suspended and that the burden of proof had effectively been reversed. In order to successfully challenge the executive freeze, the Marcoses had to essentially prove that the assets in Switzerland were the fruits of legitimate private business which of course was an impossible task. Resolution of the 'Marcos Affair' as it related to Swiss bank accounts took over twelve years of intense legal battles in Switzerland, the United States and the Philippines. The Swiss banks found themselves in a situation where their own government had assumed control over the assets while three parties tried to have the government freeze terminated: the Marcos family wanted their access restored; the Aquino administration acting through the Presidential Commission on Good Government (PCGG) was hoping to bring the Swiss accounts into the public treasury fast and lastly, a group of

inside swiss banking

some 10,000 victims of alleged human rights violations organized in a U.S. class action against the Marcos family tried to access the Swiss funds to satisfy their claim for some 2 billion dollars in exemplary and compensatory damages. The class action plaintiffs were represented by Robert A. Swift, an attorney in Philadelphia who specialized on this type of human rights litigation. We will talk about him not only in this chapter but also in the one dedicated to the Holocaust where he resurfaced a few years after the Marcos case had been resolved.

This situation of interlocked parties with irreconcilable conflicts of interest turned into a veritable nightmare for the banks that were given custody over the assets under the Swiss Government's authority. The Marcos family's pursuit of their legal options was the least complicated of them all and over the course of the 12-year saga it seemed almost as if the family became quite comfortable with the fact that as long as the executive freeze was in place, none of their adversaries in Manila or Philadelphia would be able to get access to the funds. The PCGG grew increasingly unhappy with the stalemate that the procedures around the executive freeze had turned into. While the Swiss Government took the extraordinary step of using its executive powers to lock in the Marcos assets, this was always considered a preliminary measure to ensure that the assets in question were secured in anticipation of a formal request for legal assistance in a criminal case that was being built against Ferdinand Marcos, his family and his cronies. The PCGG did in fact open a criminal case and engaged in prosecutorial investigations that led to the formal submission of a request for legal assistance in Bern shortly after the executive order had been issued. However, the judicial branch in charge of examining the merits of the legal assistance request found it lacking of substance and a tug of war ensued between Manila and Bern about what level of proof was acceptable for the legal assistance request to finally be approved and acted on. It took some four years for bank documents to be handed over to the PCGG confirming the authenticity of the 'Malacanang Documents' and eight more years for the Marcos assets to finally get transferred to the Philippines.

Meanwhile, Robert Swift prepared one of the most important cases of his career in his Philadelphia office; thousands of torture victims were interviewed in remote areas of the Philippines and affidavits were assembled to support a claim against the Marcos Estate that amounted to two billion dollars. The class action was filed in the Central District of the 9th Federal Circuit Court with the flamboyant and unpredictable judge Manuel Real presiding over the case, a veteran Federal Judge that had first been appointed by President Lyndon Johnson in 1966. Over the many years that this trial went on Swift and Real turned out to be the one pair of individuals inflicting more trouble on the Swiss banks holding the Marcos assets than everybody else

inside swiss banking

combined in the illustrious cast of characters that was brought together in the great spectacle of the Marcos Affair. It was this class action that demonstrated to the Swiss banks for the first time how aggressively the U.S. justice system will declare jurisdiction over transactions that occur beyond its borders, how relentless the U.S. legal system is in pursuing its goals and what disregard it demonstrates in cases of high priority to the sovereignty of other nations. The main problem facing the banks was that they both had significant business interest in the United States. They were prominent investment banks on Wall Street and the business generated in the United States made up a large portion of their revenues and tied up a significant portion of their balance sheets. They were exposed to the U.S. because by doing business in the United States the fell under the legal doctrine that who 'avails themselves of the United States legal system' will be subject to its rules no matter whether they are resident in the U.S. or not. The Swiss banks naturally played a large part in Robert Swift's plan to obtain access to the Marcos Estate's assets in order to satisfy his clients' claim for damages. The "Malacanang Documents" were of public record and Swift had no trouble identifying which banks Ferdinand and Imelda Marcos allegedly did business with. He also knew that the ordinary process of obtaining confirmation from Swiss judicial authorities of the existence of these accounts and their actual balances would be cumbersome. The international legal assistance process is complex and mired with the risk of interested parties interjecting appeals at various stages of the procedures. Even though it might ultimately have worked, this was clearly going to take much more time than what was acceptable to Robert Swift in his effort to get results for his clients and collect his contingency fee. After all, Robert Swift's interest in human rights could be measured in the percentage of the anticipated settlement he would be paid in compensation for his legal efforts. While Ferdinand Marcos was often nicknamed 'Mister Ten Percent' for his alleged personal cut in all government contracts, Robert Swift's pecuniary motivation in the class action was not far off. It was clearly a key driver in his relentless effort to force the Swiss banks into submission in the U.S. rather than taking the long road of a mutual assistance request in Bern. With the help of Judge Real, Mr. Swift used the U.S. branches of the Swiss banks as a lever to establish jurisdiction over the banks in the same Federal District as the Marcos Estate. What ensued was a lengthy and costly court drama in which the Swiss banks lost their case of having U.S. jurisdiction denied. At times the drama involving Real, Swift and the banks turned outright grotesque such as when Judge Real would move court hearings from Los Angeles to Honolulu, on a whim, just to cause some additional inconvenience for the New York lawyers representing the Swiss banks. This was not a friendly court and it took the intervention of the

inside swiss banking

U.S. State Department in an *amicus curiae* brief to ultimately succeed in convincing Judge Real that the road to Swiss bank documents would have to lead to Bern and not New York, Los Angeles or Honolulu.

The conflicts of interest at stake in the Marcos case made it clear after about 8 years from the initial executive freeze order that this case could potentially drag on for decades without any party obtaining any results. The Swiss Government would continue to keep the keys to the accounts and prevent the banks from giving anybody access to the money. There was clear and present danger that Judge Real would issue an order in the U.S. for the Swiss banks to pay the balances held in the Marcos accounts to the class action plaintiffs after he had awarded them close to two billion dollars in damages in 1995. This would put the banks in the impossible situation where their only choice was whether they were going to break Swiss law by complying with the U.S. court or U.S. law by complying with the Swiss government freeze. An international crisis was coming together in which the banks could not win. In addition, the banks as well as the Swiss government would get much more press and media coverage on this topic than was desirable. Neither of them wanted to be seen to be assisting the Marcos family in hanging on to their tainted wealth. As the case dragged on over the years, there was increased reputational risk to take into consideration.

After one of my colleagues at the Legal Department of Swiss Bank Corporation decided to leave the bank to pursue a career in private practice in 1994 (eight years after the Marcos assets had been frozen), I had the distinguished honour to inherit about a dozen yards worth of binders that had accumulated on my esteemed colleague's book shelf and which bore witness to the history of all the various parallel proceedings of the case. Swiss Bank was in the media frequently, defending its sitting on money that nobody in Switzerland wanted to be associated with and trying to explain the complexity of the legal situation crossing from Switzerland into the United States and ultimately to the Philippines. The longer the case dragged on the less the public would understand why the banks, Swiss Bank included, were not trying harder to get matters resolved, get rid of the Marcos assets and move on. This sentiment was shared by some of Swiss Bank's key corporate clients across Asia and the association of the bank with Marcos increasingly threatened the bank's business development success not only in the Philippines but across the region. Looking at the sheer volume of paperwork that had accumulated over the years, in combination with the growing reputational challenges and the skyrocketing legal bills, made us think whether there might be an alternative modus operandi for the 'Marcos Banks' (Swiss Bank Corporation and Credit Suisse) that would allow us all to exit gracefully from the quagmire. The

inside swiss banking

idea was as exotic as it was simple: we needed to examine what the interests were of all stakeholders in the case. They were seemingly irreconcilable because the family, the PCGG and the class action plaintiffs all wanted full access to the roughly five hundred million dollars sitting in the accounts. The Swiss government wanted its laws respected and the banks needed a framework in which they could pay out the assets without breaking any laws in Switzerland or the United States. In order to cut through the Gordian knot we needed a mechanism for dispute resolution that would bring all stakeholders around one table.

The idea of a mediation session was born, and while the two 'Marcos Banks' agreed to sponsor the process one of the key issues at the outset was to convince the Swiss Federal Government of the benefits of agreeing to an alternative dispute resolution mechanism. Governments like to operate on the basis of laws and regulations and the Swiss Federal Council had put a solid stake in the ground when they issued the executive freeze order in 1986. However, the Minister of Foreign Affairs could be convinced that the reputation of Switzerland as a financial centre would be best served by agreeing to become part of the groundbreaking mediation effort rather than stonewalling the effort by insisting on the government's sovereignty. The next step was to find a mediator that could lead the process and would be acceptable to all stakeholders. A complex search started for the appropriate person with the required diplomatic skills and proven experience in international conflict resolution. With the wide divergence of interest that existed between the Marcos family, the human rights victims, the PCGG, the banks and the Swiss government, a long list of candidates was necessary to finally find an 'A-list' personality that was not vetoed by any party. This person was Chester A. Crocker, a former senior diplomat in the George Schultz's State Department who as Assistant Secretary of State for African Affairs had been the architect of the peace process in Namibia. (A detailed account of this astonishing achievement can be found in his book "High Noon in Southern Africa: Making Peace in a Rough Neighbourhood"). His credentials were undisputable and his connection to the Reagan Administration made him acceptable to Imelda and family since it was under President Reagan that the 'soft landing' of Ferdinand Marcos in Hawaii was allowed to happen.

The Marcos Mediation took place during a week in January of 1996 in Hong Kong with a cast of characters congregating for negotiations at an undisclosed location that would have been worthy of a movie: lawyers from Switzerland and the United States, Government officials from Bern and Manila, Ferdinand 'Bambang' Marcos Jr. representing the family and Chester Crocker as Mediator. Even though the key parties were miles apart in their demands and expectations, the interest gap all but closed by

inside swiss banking

the end of the Hong Kong session. The mediation ultimately failed but it set a process in motion that created favourable conditions for the Swiss banks to achieve their goal to be able to pay out the toxic Marcos assets without breaking any laws in Switzerland or the United States. In early December of 1997, almost two years after the Marcos Mediation ended, the Class Action in the U.S. against the Swiss banks got thrown out of court. In a somewhat surprising reversal of an earlier decision by Judge Real, the US Court of Appeal in the Ninth Circuit approved the appeals brought before it by UBS and Credit Suisse and agreed with the concept that any further actions against the Swiss banks would have to be brought against them under the Swiss judicial system. Bob Swift's crusade against the Swiss "Marcos Banks" in the United States court system was over. This set the stage for the Swiss Supreme Court to render a decision in 1998 that broke the deadlock and allowed the Swiss Government to enter a deal with the Filipino Government. As a result, the frozen Marcos assets that had grown to some 650 million dollars were transferred into an escrow account under a Filipino corruption court's supervision. In 2003 the assets were released in the Philippines to fund an agrarian reform program.

'Marcos' was a groundbreaking file for the Swiss banking community on many levels. As interesting as the case was for anybody that had been involved in it, the important question to explore in the context of this book is whether the banking industry in Switzerland learned any lessons from this case and what, if any, changes were made to banking policy. The answer to both questions is affirmative. The main lesson learned was that banks had to be much more ethical in terms of the money they would accept from clients in order to make sure that they were not involuntarily getting involved in scandals down the road. Under the guidance of the Swiss Bankers Association, the framework of due diligence standards that has been in existence since 1977 was further developed and refined. It just recently went through another revision in 2008 and has been the backbone of Swiss banks' code of conduct. We will explore the Code of Due Diligence in further detail later on. No matter how diligent a bank is in making sure they know the identity of their clients this level of diligence alone has proven to be inefficient in terms of fending off involvement in financial scandals later on. What the Marcos case demonstrated like no other before it was that as ethical standards of behaviour change so does the risk profile of the bank. When Ferdinand Marcos first opened the accounts at the banks in Switzerland nobody was overly concerned about dealing with a dictator with questionable integrity. More importantly, nobody thought it important to verify the source of the assets that were transferred to the banks to make sure they were in fact dealing with the family's private fortune and not with money that should have remained with the Filipino treasury. The banks'

inside swiss banking

philosophy in these days was one of 'see no evil, hear no evil'. Bank regulations in terms of determining the legitimacy of client assets were very loose if not inexistent. Money laundering was not part of a banker's vocabulary. The was no rule book to determine what to do if a world-known politician like Marcos moves through stages from being globally respected to being tolerated, then openly criticized and ultimately thrown out of office by his own people. At what stage should a bank decide to increase its vigilance vis-à-vis this type of client? When would it be appropriate to determine that the client relationship was no longer viable and therefore had to be terminated?

By far the most important lesson learned from the Marcos case was that politicians were a client category that needed to be treated with heightened scrutiny and attention. Political power has the potential to bring the best and worst out in any person that runs for office. Marcos is only one example of many and we don't necessarily have to veer off to far corners of the globe to find corruption and misdirection of public funds. The most effective way to limit a bank's risk of being involved in a politician's business when corruption charges materialize is to set stringent rules determining under which circumstances a bank is prepared to engage in a business relationship with this client category in the first place. 'Marcos' has initiated the process of establishing client acceptance policies regarding so-called 'politically exposed persons' or PEPs.

PEPs are generally defined as individuals with a political mandate in a senior position with any branch of government: judicial, legislative or executive and the policy restrictions include their extended families. Account openings for PEPs require the approval of a member of senior executive management and as part of the approval process the bank will insist on documentation supporting the fact that the assets placed with the bank have a source that is not connected to the political mandate. If an existing client falls under the PEP definition sometime during the banking relationship, senior executive management will ensure that the relationship goes through a full PEP assessment and a decision is made whether to continue the relationship or not. Not only are these PEP rules an important part of internal policy setting under a banks' own discretion; they have become the standard of care under FATF guidelines and the regulatory audit framework. The fight against corruption has become a high priority issue globally as organizations like the OECD have increased their focus on the influence of criminal organizations in a globalized economy. While different cultural or religious belief systems will always influence the prevalent views on legal and ethical standards in specific parts of the world, it is widely recognized that the phenomenon of corruption needs to be singled out as one of the major barriers to creating global prosperity and security. By virtue of money being at the centre of all corruption activity, the global

inside swiss banking

banking industry cannot escape being involved in this debate. As the global regulatory and legal framework has adapted to the challenges of money laundering, organized crime and corruption, banks are now part of a much improved regulatory environment designed to ensure that money flows are tracked and criminal activity is detected, reported and prosecuted on a local and global scale. 'Marcos' would not be possible in today's framework of international regulation of financial services.

CHAPTER SEVEN

Smell Tests and Reputational Pitfalls

Another lesson learned from 'Marcos' is that banks found their reputation attacked because their process lacked attention to simple 'smell tests' when it came to accepting clients or auditing existing clients' banking business. Measured by today's standards of conduct, Ferdinand and Imelda Marcos would likely not have passed the initial 'smell test' when they established a business relationship with the banks, irrespective of whether or not the banks had PEP policies in place. One could easily argue that Marcos was always shrouded in a cloud of discomfort with regards to his exercising political power. There was a reason why he was nick-named 'Mister Ten Percent' and this was a well known fact early in his political career. There was plenty of smell surrounding his financial affairs at any time and the 'Marcos banks' could have spared themselves a significant amount of financial and reputational expense had they refused to do business with the man from Manila in the first place.

inside swiss banking

In my career as legal counsel at Swiss Bank Corporation in the 1980s and 1990s I came across a plethora of situations where my own standards of smell test could not be satisfied. The question in my mind was less whether the bank was technically exposed to legal risk or not in dealing with certain customers or executing certain transactions. The key question was whether doing so would expose us to unacceptable reputational risks. The then Chairman of Swiss Bank set a very simple standard defining his expectation of how bank executives should make decisions: If a transaction we were involved in should put the bank into media headlines, would we be proud of it or feel ashamed. This was as simple a guideline as it was powerful, even though it left a gap in defining acceptable corporate behaviour. The decision where to draw the line was driven by individual perceptions and by a changing environment rather than strict bank guidelines.

The late 1980s and the 1990s in particular were a fascinating period to be involved in private banking in Switzerland. As discussed earlier in the book, this was the period in which insider trading became a criminal offence and anti-money-laundering rules were introduced. Client disclosure rules were tightened and transparency in business conduct increased. The banks could no longer go about their business following the ancient Roman axiom of 'pecunia non olet' (money does not smell) and therefore adopt the somewhat abstract notion that money by itself was removed from the classical ethical dilemmas of right or wrong, good or bad. The evolving doctrine was that anything involving money had a smell; good or bad, tolerable or not. Deciding what types of banking activities would be acceptable became much more an ethical process than a determination of legal risks. The Chairman's headline test became a useful proxy in the exercise of resolving omnipresent ethical dilemmas. It led to executives erring on the side of caution to a higher degree than what could be witnessed recently, most visibly in the case UBS is facing in the U.S. for conspiracy to tax evasion and providing investment advice in the U.S. without required licenses. The case surrounding UBS' offshore business in the United States demonstrates the validity of the headline test rather drastically. Would the UBS executives have asked themselves what the probable outcome would be for the bank if the business with U.S. clients offshore were to make it to the headlines not only in print media but on the internet? Would the business practices have been modified? The answer to this somewhat rhetorical question would obviously have to come from UBS and in the context of this discussion we can leave the answer open. What the UBS case in the U.S. also demonstrates radically is that a reputation that has been built, maintained and nurtured over decades can be destroyed in a second. This has been true for decades, where the media consisted mainly of newspapers, magazines, radio and TV. It is magnified today

inside swiss banking

through the impact of the internet and the dramatic changes it has brought, not only to how information is distributed, but how discussions on news will be augmented by blogs and chat rooms. In the internet age the headline risk spins out of control and there is little anybody can do to contain it. As a result, the task of restoring reputational damage by controlling the message and the spin has become an infinitely more difficult challenge today than what it was two or three decades ago.

UBS is an unfortunate but good example to make this point. Both the firm and its former Chairman used to be icons of international success. Under the leadership of Marcel Ospel UBS became a true global leader and innovator of financial services. The acquisition of Paine Webber in 2000 made UBS a significant player in the U.S., not only in investment banking but also in retail distribution through one of the largest broker networks in the country. Together with the largest franchise in global private banking and leadership positions in investment banking in Europe and Asia, the increased reach in the U.S. made UBS the undisputed number one in Swiss banking and earned Marcel Ospel the title of Switzerland's most influential and respected business leader in 2007. But then the sub-prime crisis hit the world and UBS was faced with having to write off amounts in excess of forty billion dollars in value adjustments. UBS was by far the hardest hit European bank and had a lot of explaining to do as this kind of

57

adventurous behaviour seemed untypical for a Swiss bank that prided itself of being a leader in global risk management. In the aftermath of the first round of write-offs the bank published an epic 'mea culpa' report explaining what went wrong. UBS openly admitted that the obsession of the management board with competing with the leading U.S. investment banks in the fixed income sector had fatally clouded their judgement. As a result, unreasonable risks were taken, and warnings by internal controls ignored, in building up trading positions in what later became the culprit for the largest write-down in history. In order to survive the mayhem in the sub-prime disaster as well as the subsequent market meltdown UBS had to raise capital numerous times. The situation was so desperate in fact, that the bank ultimately had to take the previously unimaginable step of asking the Swiss government to step in with a six billion Swiss Franc bailout in the form of convertible subordinated debt. In addition, a Central Bank funded vehicle was created to purchase up to sixty billion Swiss Francs worth of toxic assets to clear the bank's balance sheet. After all had been said and done, UBS was no different than Citibank, Merrill Lynch and the many other prominent US banks and investment firms that had to be bailed out by Washington. Even though it was the logical consequence of UBS desperately trying to compete with the madness on Wall Street, it nevertheless surprised those who up to then believed that Swiss banks were safer than any other financial institution in the world. The reputational damage created by the misguided fixed income adventure of UBS was massive, especially with respect to its private banking division. Existing and prospective clients alike became confused as to the bank's ability to protect their wealth. Clients took a run on the bank that resulted in massive outflows of several billions of dollars in assets under management in 2008 and 2009. The bank also had clearly visible difficulties generating new business as clients were no longer naturally attracted to UBS after the significant loss in its reputation as a reliable world leader in private banking. The frustrating part for the private banking division within UBS was that the private bank would pay a hefty price for the hit to the firm's reputation even though it was the investment bank that created the problem in the first place through its misguided fixed income growth strategy. With its previously stellar reputation scratched, the bank became increasingly vulnerable to attacks. The most prominent and public of which was of the course the U.S. Senate inquiry in alleged conspiracy with clients who are violating U.S. tax laws. This topic developed a life of its own and compounded the reputational hit that UBS had taken in the sub-prime debacle. It will be explored in detail in one of the following chapters. In an ever-changing world of ethical standards and best practices Swiss banks will find no shortage of opportunities to adapt their sensory for smells and reputational pitfalls. Most of them had their fair share of exposure in past decades. The stage is set in the current tax debate in the United States and across the European Union for future challenges to which the banks on the shores of Lakes Zurich, Geneva and Lugano will have to adapt.

inside swiss banking

CHAPTER EIGHT

Swiss Banks and the Holocaust

It was a sunny afternoon on a December day in Washington D.C. in 1995. The United States Capital had just gone through a major snow storm the day before. I remember to this day walking through inches of fresh snow at night on my way back to the Four Seasons Hotel in Georgetown. The snow made everything so peaceful and quiet; it felt like Switzerland where I had arrived from the day before. On that sunny afternoon I was sitting in a law office in downtown Washington preparing the Marcos mediation with Chester Crocker. As we were wrapping things up, the mediator's legal counsel asked me to step up to the window to enjoy the view from the 20th floor over the D.C. core, the Washington Monument and Capitol Hill. Then she pointed out a specific building and asked me whether I knew what building it was. I did not, as my last sightseeing tour of D.C. had been in 1978 and I had not memorized more than the obvious landmarks. The mystery building was the Library of Congress and the reason why counsel singled the building out as we were gazing across

61

the D.C. skyline was the work Senator Alphonse D'Amato was busy with in its halls. D'Amato was building a case against the Swiss banking system with regards to dormant accounts held for Holocaust victims. Early indications in the Washington inner circles were that the Senator from New York was on to highly explosive discoveries that would come as a broadside against the Swiss. The reputational and legal issues we were dealing with in the Marcos case would be 'peanuts' against what was brewing in the Library of Congress. As legal counsel for SBC I knew that the Swiss government had dealt with Holocaust assets in the early 1960s. A a federal order required all banks holding assets for known Holocaust victims to surrender these assets into the custody of the Swiss National Bank which then turned the total of the reported assets over to Israel. The assumption within the Swiss banking industry was that the Swiss banks' exposure to the Holocaust had long been dealt with. But my friends in Washington insisted that we would be well advised to dig deeper in order to be prepared when Senator D'Amato was going public with his findings. Upon my return to Switzerland I dutifully submitted my D.C. intelligence report to the Chairman and the CEO of the bank. As I expected, the reaction was to refer to the transfers of the 1960s rather than engaging in a preparatory internal investigation of what might not have been covered by the government orders over 30 years ago. As it turned out later on, the issue was that the federal order

inside swiss banking

in the 1960s only covered known victims of the Holocaust. Thousands of account of unknown victims of the Third Reich still existed with Swiss banks. So SBC, as well as all the other banks, kept sitting on accounts that were connected to the Holocaust, waiting for Alphonse D'Amato to come out with his report and start an inquiry. Nobody had claimed rights to these accounts for several years, if not decades and there was no contact between the banks and the account holders or their appointed powers of attorney. In Swiss banking terminology they were called "dormant account". It is unclear whether such internal inquiries into dormant accounts at Swiss banks would have changed the outcome of the Holocaust case in the United States and the ultimate settlement that was reached in 1999. In retrospect, however, it seems as though following the lead we got on that clear December afternoon in Washington would at least have given the banks a better shot at being prepared when D'Amato hit them in 1996. An opportunity presented itself to the banks, the Swiss Bankers Association and the Swiss Government, to make use of the advance notice we received in December of 1995 to develop a unified position towards the allegations and the negative spin that D'Amato would present to the world media, but nobody saw a reason to act pre-emptively. From the Swiss point of view the Holocaust issue had been dealt with collaboratively and in a constructive way in the 1960s and there was a notion that the U.S. Senate could not possibly come forward with new

63

information and intelligence that would suggest otherwise. Unfortunately this turned out to be a somewhat misguided approach to what was coming.

The Holocaust case against Switzerland as a nation and against the Swiss banks in particular became a legal nightmare and a media disaster in a very short time span. The investigation into Holocaust victim accounts at Swiss banks started in 1996 and ramped up to become one of the most significant public relations issues the Swiss financial sector and Switzerland as a nation had ever been faced with. At the centre of the investigation were dormant accounts. The issue of dormant accounts is not specific to Holocaust victims; as we have seen, these are simply accounts where the bank did not have actual contact with the account holder or persons with powers of attorney for a long period of time. No deposits or withdrawals had been made; no direct contact had been established either by phone or in person. Banks in every financial centre around the globe have policies and procedures in place to deal with dormant accounts. In fact, the vast majority of jurisdictions require banks by law to transfer dormant accounts to the Central Bank after a certain period of time. This is not the case in Switzerland where there is no statute of limitations for bank accounts that have gone dormant. A Swiss bank will therefore have client accounts on its books for perpetuity if these accounts do not get claimed by the account holder or their successors or powers of attorney at

inside swiss banking

some point. This lack of a statute whereby accounts will have to be handed over to the Central Bank after say 10 years of going dormant is one of the specific Swiss rules that made the situation in Switzerland uniquely interesting for families of Holocaust victims to claim forgotten assets. The other one is the fact that under Swiss law powers of attorney given by one person to another will survive the death or incapacity of the person granting the power of attorney. Unlike in most other jurisdictions, powers of attorney will not be voided by the death of the account holder. As a result, holders of a power of attorney will be able to withdraw assets held in the name of the principal account holder at any time. We will get back to the phenomenon of powers of attorney in the context of the Holocaust in a bit.

If Switzerland would have established a statutory transfer of dormant assets to the Swiss National Bank (SNB) anytime after World War II, all 'forgotten' assets held by Swiss banks for victims of the Holocaust would have been held centrally by the SNB, together with all other dormant accounts from the same time period. In all likelihood these assets would have been included in the Holocaust transfer of assets to Israel in the 1960s and there would not have been a case against the Swiss banks for Senator D'Amato to put together. Unfortunately for the Swiss, the fact that banks had to keep custody over dormant accounts in perpetuity played against them as they

65

had to account for what kinds of Holocaust related assets formed part of their dormant accounts. Even though the assets had to be kept segregated in perpetuity, the statutory obligation to keep records of banking transactions is limited at ten years. As a result, the banks would in many cases only know who the original account holder was but there would not be any records of transactions based on which deposits and withdrawals could be traced for time periods before, during and after World War II. Some banks would destroy documents after keeping records for ten years, others kept documents on file longer but there was no consistency in terms of what types of transaction records were still available. The situation was confusing to say the least. The banks took the initial position that all Holocaust related accounts had long been liquidated under the 1960 legislation and that there were no dormant Holocaust accounts left in the first place. But nobody really knew because the record keeping was not organized so that Holocaust clients would be kept separate from all other accounts dating back to the 1930s and 40s. Granted, one could assume from last names and maybe from country of residence found in the basic account documents whether someone was Jewish and potentially exposed to the horrors of the Holocaust. However, in German speaking Europe a person with the name Grossmann could be Jewish or not, Stauffenberg might sound like a Jewish name in North America but in fact the most famous Stauffenberg in

inside swiss banking

Germany was a member of the German Wehrmacht that tried unsuccessfully to assassinate Hitler in 1944. In other words, identifying potential Holocaust victims from the account documentation was not as easy as it might seem at first glance.

When Senator D'Amato and the Senate Banking Committee started their crusade against Switzerland the country and its banking industry were largely unprepared. As mentioned earlier the first official reaction from Bern was that all Holocaust related issues had been dealt with more than 30 years ago and that there was nothing left to discuss. Unfortunately the Swiss had not done their homework. D'Amato's Senate Banking committee would continuously feed bits and pieces of information on possible Holocaust related accounts held at Swiss banks. Swiss authorities first denied the authenticity only to confirm the committee's views after a more thorough examination of the presented evidence. What ensued was continuous back-pedaling by the Swiss in which one concession was made after another. The Senate hearings were by far not the only problem facing the Swiss government and banking industry. In parallel to these hearings, several class action suits were launched in New York against Swiss banks and other institutions alleging Swiss cooperation with Nazi Germany by 'knowingly concealing and retaining assets of Holocaust victims and by accepting and laundering illegally obtained Nazi loot and profits of slave labour'. These were damaging allegations against a nation that kept its neutrality intact throughout the Nazi Regime and created a safe haven for many Jewish families that were persecuted by the Nazis. The double impact from the U.S. Senate and the class action in New York hit the Swiss psyche at its core. In order to deal with these allegations outside of the courtroom two separate investigative commissions were created. The Volcker Committee, under the leadership of former Federal Reserve Chairman Paul Volcker, was formed by way of Memorandum of Understanding between the Swiss Bankers Association, the World Jewish Congress and the World Jewish Restitution Organization in May of 1996. The Bergier Commission was established in December 1996 by the Swiss Parliament to examine the role of Switzerland in facilitating money flows for Nazi Germany between 1933 and 1945 and the immediate period after the War ended.

In connection with the Swiss banking industry two significant events stand out in this period of heated debate in court rooms and international politics. Let us look at the class actions first. As mentioned in the chapter dedicated to Ferdinand Marcos, Robert A. Swift who had gathered a large amount of knowledge and expertise about how to obtain Swiss bank documents in a court case filed in a U.S. court joined the team of counsel representing the thousands of Holocaust victims brought together under various classes. All the separately filed class actions were

inside swiss banking

ultimately consolidated under the purview of one judge in New York. After battling the Swiss 'Marcos Banks' for years, Robert Swift found a second calling in this case. The task of finding Swiss accounts for the thousands of class plaintiffs was obviously much more difficult than what Swift had faced in the Marcos case where he had access to the 'Malacanang Documents' listing all alleged Swiss accounts and providing copies of bank documents. In the case of the Holocaust victims there was no such luck and it would take a gargantuan effort to gain access to bank records if the existence of bank accounts wasn't even certain. Even so, the class action plaintiffs had a powerful ally in the U.S. Senate . Through the inquiry into the role of Switzerland with regards to the Holocaust and its interactions with Nazi Germany the U.S. Senate had put enormous pressure on the Swiss Government to find answers and cooperate with the U.S. in order to restore its international credibility and reputation. While the class action law suit took its course in New York the Swiss banks and government had an even bigger problem in the court of public opinion. The Volcker Commission was hard at work pulling together binders full of documents to establish how many bank accounts had been opened for possible Holocaust victims between 1933 and 1945. But given the enormous pressure that the Swiss banks saw themselves exposed to, they pushed for a settlement in the class action over a year before the Volcker Commission published its final report. As per this settlement of August 1998 the Swiss banks paid the staggering amount of 1.25 billion US dollars to various Jewish organizations to be distributed according to the recommendations made by the Volcker Committee at a later date. These recommendations were included in the Committee's final report in December of 1999. A list of some 21,000 names of potential Holocaust victim account holders was published, an absolute first in Swiss banking history. A click on the designated website was all it took to find out whether a relative that passed away in a Concentration Camp had managed to move some rainy day money safely into Switzerland before being apprehended by the Nazis. For a banking system that is built on privacy and confidentiality this was a truly unusual way to resolve the issue. The total amount of assets 'probably' and 'possibly' linked to Holocaust victims was tacked at somewhere between $643 million and $1.36 billion. The settlement offered a year earlier turned out to be in the ballpark even though there was no certainty in the Volcker numbers. As one can easily imagine, finding the dormant accounts that had been opened between 1933 and 1945 was the easy part. After all, these accounts had remained in the custody of the banks and the basic documents revealing the names of the account holders or people otherwise connected to the accounts by way of powers of attorney or signatory rights still existed. The difficulty was in assessing whether these interested parties

inside swiss banking

had been in fact exposed to the Holocaust. In doing so the Commission had to adopt liberal standards for documentary evidence. As one might imagine the usual documents such as death certificates and probate certificates were not obtainable in these cases. Insisting in claimants submitting documentary evidence of their relatives' passing during the Holocaust would have been sheer sarcasm and the same was true with regards to documents supporting their rights to a deceased Holocaust victim's estate.

While the original claims made in the consolidated class actions amounted to some $20 billion the settlement between the banks and the Jewish organizations was for only six percent of the claim. This constitutes an enormous discrepancy between claim and settlement, even for U.S. class action standards. Why did the claimants believe there was so much more money hidden in Swiss bank accounts and why was their intelligence so out of touch with realities? We will most likely never know for sure as the court case has been settled and people move on. However, there are some explanations as to why there was so much less money left at Swiss banks than what the Jewish organizations had expected to find. Firstly, we need to go back to the legalities around powers of attorney which, as explained earlier survive the principal's death. In order to make sure that assets which had been moved to safety in Switzerland were accessible to relatives escaping

71

the Holocaust, account holders will have almost routinely appointed powers of attorney. The individuals designated under a power of attorney would have had unlimited access to the accounts and we will never really know how many accounts had been disposed of or significantly drawn on by the designated persons. It is entirely possible to imagine though that a significant portion of the assets moved to safety have disappeared this way over time, both during the war and after as it became clear that the principal account holders had been killed. Secondly, not all accounts would have been set up in the names of the person trying to put money in a safe place. People were extremely cautious about revealing identities and nobody could be sure as to how long Switzerland could withstand the risk of an invasion by the Nazis in which case their assets would have been found out. It is therefore not unrealistic to think that accounts would have been opened in the names of nominees and by lawyers and other professional fiduciaries acting as principals in order to protect their clients. This all took place some 40 to 50 years before the full disclosure rules were introduced and the financial industry started to worry about money laundering and inadvertently dealing with organized crime or terrorist organizations. These nominees, lawyers and other representatives of Holocaust victims may have made good use of the money placed in the custody of Swiss banks during and immediately after the war. Since most of the transaction records had been destroyed years ago, there is no way to know for sure what happened in all the accounts. We elaborated earlier about the ten year record keeping requirements which would indicate that most records of transaction that occurred during the war or in the immediate time period after would in fact have been destroyed in the 1960s. How was it then that the Volcker Commission could reconstruct so many accounts and determine that some 21,000 accounts may be categorized as holding Holocaust related assets? The simple answer is that the ten year record keeping requirement did not mean that records actually had to be destroyed after ten years and most banks in fact kept records much longer than the required ten years. Given the explosiveness around the Holocaust accounts the Swiss Federal Banking Commission (SFBC) issued an order early in the process of dealing with the allegations made by the U.S. Senate that no bank was allowed to destroy any documents relating to events that occurred in the sensitive time period. The ten year statute was declared out of force as far as bank documents were concerned. The Swiss Government needed to make sure that no potentially incriminating documents would disappear at the eleventh hour if the efforts of the Volcker and Bernier Commissions were to be taken seriously. But not every bank felt the urge to comply with the SFBC order. One night in January 1997, a night guard working at Union Bank of Switzerland in Zurich discovered large amounts of old documents dating back to the time of

World War II or even earlier in a bin ready to be shredded the next day. Christoph Meili, the brave night guard blew the whistle, decided to remove some of the documents from the shredding queue and handed them over to a Jewish organization in Zurich. Union Bank was furious as it had been found out in its efforts to illegally destroy what might have been embarrassing or even incriminating evidence. Meili had broken the law in Switzerland by making the documents available to a third party rather than calling the police. The Swiss were equally outraged at both, the largest bank in the country for having the arrogance to believe they could get away with illegally destroying documentary evidence of their involvement in transactions with Nazi Germany as well as Christoph Meili for handing over the documents to a Jewish organization rather than the Swiss authorities. Senator D'Amato and Ed Fagan, the lead counsel in the U.S. class action, however, were delighted at the 'chutzpah' demonstrated by Meili. Fagan sued UBS on behalf of Meili for the exaggerated amount of 2.5 billion dollars and upon intervention from the Senator Meili became the first and only Swiss citizen that had ever been granted political asylum in the United States. Meili's case became part of the overall Holocaust settlement. He still lives in the State of California but his cozy relationship with Ed Fagan and the Jewish organizations allegedly came to an end as it appeared that his expectation of receiving significant compensation for his efforts was somewhat disappointed.

Switzerland' involvement with Nazi Germany and the Holocaust has been documented for future historians to study. The Volcker and Bernier Commissions have delivered invaluable insights into how the tiny neutral country South of Germany tried to survive by facilitating Nazi business at the same time assets were kept safe for Jewish families that were deported and killed by the Nazis. Senator Alphonse D'Amato has shed light on how the Swiss acted to survive under the threat of annihilation by Hitler and the Holocaust claims have left an indelible mark on how Switzerland and its banks are perceived by the international community. But most importantly the U.S. based Holocaust initiatives have forced the Swiss as a nation as well as its financial services industry to deal with their past. What resulted is a Swiss national conscience that has a clear understanding of the nation's role during the darkest time in recent European history and a banking system that has cleared the clouds of doubt regarding its dealings with Nazi Germany on the one hand and Holocaust victims on the other. The quick settlement of the class action claims undoubtedly helped in restoring normalcy in the Swiss banking sector faster than anybody would have anticipated and what started as a media and public opinion nightmare turned out as an opportunity for Switzerland to clean the slate.

CHAPTER NINE

The Twin Towers

Up until 9-11-2001 nobody in their right mind would have imagined that there would come a day in which four commercial passenger airplanes would be used by terrorists as weapons of mass destruction. We all vividly remember the images of the Twin Towers of what used to be the World Trade Center in Lower Manhattan collapsing after 2 airplanes had been flown into them in a suicide mission performed by Al-Qaeda. We equally remember the pictures of the damage created at the Pentagon and the heroic acts of a few passengers traveling in the fourth plane that caused it to crash in a field in Pennsylvania en route to the White House. On September 11, 2001 terrorism had made its brutal entry into North American reality. This was a new sensation that has altered the mindset of America. While the attacks of 9-11 were unmatched in their brutality, other parts of the world had experienced the effects of terror decades earlier as in the 1970s and 80s the Irish Republican Army had left its unmistakable mark on London's Charing Cross Tube station, the Baader Meinhof

inside swiss banking

Group terrorised Germany and the Italian city of Bologna witnessed devastating attacks by the Red Brigades on its main train station. But unlike the IRA, Baader Meinhof or Italy's Red Brigade, Al Qaeda is a global organization and on 9-11 it proved to the world that it had reach anywhere it wanted with devastating effect not only on the people their attacks would kill but on the global economic system. A hit on New York and Washington was not only useful for its symbolism but for the disruption it would create in the markets. It would demonstrate to the world how vulnerable the world's leading political and economic powerhouse was after all.

9-11 had far reaching consequences on how the United States looked at the potential for future aggression against the sovereignty, integrity and basic value system the nation stands for. This was only the third time since the Proclamation of Independence that the U.S. had been attacked by a foreign entity on her soil. But unlike the Japanese hit on the U.S. Navy in Pearl Harbour or the Loyalists from British North America burning down the White House during the War of 1812, this was the first attack on the United States on her own soil outside of an actual War. In the aftermath of 9-11 the U.S. tightened her borders, introduced biometric identification of individuals at border crossings, created the Department of Homeland Security, marched into Afghanistan in the hopes of catching Osama Bin Laden and put together a case to finish the job in Iraq. None of these measures had a direct impact on how global financial services are conducted and how they interact with the U.S.; but the introduction of the Patriot Act did. The USA Patriot Act was passed by Congress on October 26, 2001, less than two months after the attacks on the Twin Towers. The acronym actually has a meaning much more specific than simple patriotism. It stands for 'Uniting and Strengthening America by Providing Appropriate Tools Required to Intercept and Obstruct Terrorism'. The Bush Administration and Congress were under pressure to find an appropriate reaction to the acts of terrorism committed in New York and Arlington. It is impressive that some dedicated soul in the U.S. Congress actually took the time in all the confusion and hastiness to come up with an acronym that would rally the American public to pass a piece of legislation that for the purpose of fighting terrorism gave up large parts of the very civil liberties the United Stated had been built on. The Patriot Act gave wider powers to intelligence and law enforcement to tap into private conversations, to detain and deport immigrants suspected of terrorist activity, and many more restrictions on traditional civil liberties that made the U.S. a beacon of liberty for the rest of the world. In terms of financial services, the Patriot Act introduced new levels of control with regards to the movement of money globally and in the U.S. It also increased client identification rules. In order to ensure that all financial transactions of

inside swiss banking

individuals suspected of terrorist connections could be traced, continuously updated lists of individuals were introduced that financial institutions dealing with the U.S. are required to consult on a regular basis. Reporting rules were introduced for any financial institution that had contact with any of the individuals contained on this list. Banks and other financial institutions de facto became a branch of a virtual global financial police. If a person had the wrong last name and happened to have been in the wrong place at the wrong time, they would not be able to engage in financial transactions with any reputable bank as they would be caught by the Anti-Terrorism list. But even for individuals or companies without any connections to the list, the Patriot Act has changed the rules. Under the Patriot Act, banks are now required to identify not only the account holder but also any individuals beneficially interested in the account. If companies are used to hold personal assets, there is heightened scrutiny and the rules that Switzerland introduced regarding dealings with politically exposed persons was refined and extended. The fight against the ever growing network of unrelenting Islamic terrorists has increased the need of any bank dealing with the U.S. directly or indirectly to massively increase their compliance departments. Banks around the world, including Swiss banks had to redefine the way they do business to satisfy a new legislative and regulatory framework established in the U.S. that was designed for maximum impact against organized crime and terrorism. The somewhat disproportioned encroachment on the confidentiality and privacy normally afforded to law abiding bank customers became collateral damage in the War On Terror as defined by the Bush Administration. President George W. Bush made to things unequivocally clear in his first address to Congress and the world after 9-11: The U.S. considered itself at war against Al Qaeda and in his black and white view of things nations all over the globe had to make a choice to either be with the U.S. or be considered an enemy. This choice extended to compliance with the Patriot Act and thus changed the way the world does its banking, simply because any bank in the world will at some point transact through the U.S. and therefore be affected by the Patriot Act and the regulations based on it. The spread of terrorism in the early part of the new millennium has changed the way financial business gets transacted much in the same way as it has changed the way people travel. Today there is a global banking equivalent to taking off ones shoes, belt and watch when going though security and to being inconvenienced by the limitations on toiletries and liquids one can bring on board a commercial airliner. Execution of financial transactions requires a much enlarged degree of disclosure today than what was common practice before the Patriot Act came into effect. Privacy conscious bank clients find it virtually impossible to hide behind a personal investment company or other corporate structures where the identity of the individual controlling the directors could remain unknown. These were common practices in many jurisdictions before October 2001 and have now been shut down. There is no such thing as an undisclosed principal in financial transactions in the post 9-11 world. This creates some minor inconvenience to some clients but overall it has actually increased the reliability of financial markets as it made it infinitely more difficult not only for terrorists but also for 'normal' organized crime to abuse the global financial system.

As we have explored earlier in the book, Switzerland had introduced some of the most stringent client identification and transactional due diligence rules during the early 1990s. As such, the Swiss financial services sector was ahead of the curve when it had to adapt to the provisions of the Patriot Act. Registration of individuals with a beneficial interest in accounts held by third parties was a requirement in Switzerland long before it was introduced in the U.S. in 2001 as part of the ordinary conduct of banking business. The Anti-Money-Laundering (AML) laws established in Switzerland in 1990 introduced specific rules for banks to report suspicious client behaviour to the authorities and a specific government agency was established to receive and manage reports made under the AML regulations. The Swiss were a leading jurisdiction in this area before 2001 and only small changes had to be made to bank policies and procedures in order to satisfy the requirements of the Patriot Act. The increased level of U.S. involvement in global policing of money laundering and terrorist financing activity just added some complexities in terms of asserting Swiss sovereignty over the information collected under AML and Patriot Act provisions. Any nation that wanted to be part of the international community that was 'with the United States" rather than against it, had to find ways to facilitate the flow of information gathered under local AML laws and the Patriot Act, across borders into the U.S. This obviously was a challenge to Switzerland with its tight bank secrecy laws. But the handling by the Swiss of their obligations under the Patriot Act never caused any concern in the U.S. because protocols for the exchange of information in the fight against money laundering and terrorist financing were easier to put in place than for the exchange of tax information, as we will explore in much more detail later. In the global fight against terrorist financing and organized crime the issue of dual incrimination, one of the key issues in tax matters, does not come up.

CHAPTER TEN

Swiss Banks' Code of Due Diligence

We have already touched on the Code of Due Diligence (CDB) that all Swiss banks have agreed to submit themselves to under the guidance and supervision of the Swiss Bankers' Association (SBA). The CDB serves as the framework of business standards in terms of client identification and generally accepted business practices. It contains self-regulating and audit provisions with sanctions against member banks that are found in violation of the agreement and as such has proven to be an effective self-regulating tool for the SBA not only to set but to enforce best business practices. Compliance with the provisions of the CDB will also serve as one of the tests that the Swiss federal banking regulators will apply in auditing the business conduct of banks.

The CDB has first been put in place in 1977 as a response of the banking industry to questionable practices that occurred at the Chiasso branch of Credit Suisse. Chiasso is a small town in the South of Switzerland bordering Italy with a population of fifteen thousand. The size of the town is disproportionate to the importance that Chiasso had for the numerous Swiss banks that had a branch there in the 1970s. These branches did not primarily serve the local population; they were set up to deal with Italian clients bringing money across the border for a variety of reasons, such as to keep it safe from political turmoil, corruption and the Mafia. Some eager managers at the Credit Suisse branch had engaged in assisting some of their Italian clients in illegally exporting Italian currency into Switzerland. They also actively assisted their clients in using corporate structures in Liechtenstein to hide the true identity of the Italian clients. These structures were used to reinvest the assets back into the Italian economy on a virtually anonymous basis. Italian clients used the confidentiality offered by Switzerland's banks and the company laws in the tiny Principality of Liechtenstein to roundtrip assets back into the Italian economy. The anonymous re-investment scheme went bad when the Italian Lira began to fall significantly against other major currencies, including the Swiss Franc, and the Italian export industry started suffering as a result. The investments made through the Liechtenstein vehicles lost most of their value and at least one of these Liechtenstein companies was bound for bankruptcy. To complicate matters even more, senior executives at the Chiasso branch had issued a guarantee covering the Liechtstein investments that were recycled into the Italian economy. At the time, they did not understand how significant the credit risk of this transaction would turn out to be. On the other hand, they likely knew that securing the transaction with a bank facility was not entirely within bank policy, which is why they issued the guarantee without approvals from head office. The chiefs in Zurich did not have to know all the details of the intricate cross-border business that the southern-most branch engaged in. When the reinvestment company went under and the guarantee was called, Credit Suisse incurred a loss of over one billion Swiss Francs. 30 years ago this was an enormous number. The banking industry had not yet gotten used to billions of write-downs as they became ubiquitous in 2008. Credit Suisse survived the hit to its bottom line but at the cost of significant reputational damage. The Chiasso executives were put behind bars and a thorough investigation of what happened in Chiasso ensued both on the part of the SBA and the SFBC. Interestingly, the illegal export of Italian currency by Italian nationals was not primarily designed to evade tax in Italy. The motivation was to bring money to safety in Switzerland out of concern that the Italian Communist Party might imminently rise to power. The regulatory issue behind the transfer was that Credit Suisse representatives assumed an active role in exporting the currency across the border and reinvesting the money back into Italy through the Liechtenstein vehicle. By doing so they assisted the clients in violating Italian exchange control laws. The Chiasso Affair resulted in an overhaul of senior ranks within Credit Suisse right up to head office and it spurred the introduction of an industry-wide code of due diligence under the guidance of the SBA. The 1977 version of the code became the "Agreement on the Swiss banks' code of conduct with regard to the exercise of due diligence" (short: "CDB") which is binding for all members of the Swiss Bankers Association. It has been revised and adapted to the constant change in the financial regulatory environment in a five-year cycle since it first got introduced over 30 years ago. The most recent version of the CDB has come into force in 2008.

The CDB pursues the mission of 'preserving the good name of the Swiss banking community', establishing best practices in business conduct and 'making an effective contribution to combating money laundering and terrorist financing'. The main sections of the CDB are dedicated to the identification of contracting parties and of the 'beneficial owners' of the assets deposited with the banks, as well as the prohibition to actively assist in the flight of capital and tax evasion. The CDB further contains provisions about how violations of the rules contained therein shall be sanctioned to ensure that the member banks have a strong incentive to enforce the CDB within their organizations. The CDB rules also serve as best practice standard that law enforcement and criminal prosecutors will rely on when examining the activities of a bank or their executives and employees with regards to

inside swiss banking

possible infractions of the Anti-Money Laundering Act and respective regulations.

Verification of the identity of contracting parties is one of the key objectives of the CDB. Knowing who your client is lies at the heart of the fight against money laundering as well as the endeavour to avoid doing business with clients that may potentially expose the banks to undue reputational risks. For this reason the CDB has established a host of rules and guidelines pertaining to how account holders have to be identified. The rules are straightforward when the account holder is also the person with the beneficial interest in the assets. It gets more complex in the case of accounts held by offshore corporations or trusts where the contracting party is not the person with the beneficial interest. In such cases, Swiss banks will have to take any reasonable steps required of them to ascertain who in fact the person or group is standing behind the formal account holder and exercising control over the assets. Imagine Samuel Jones, the sole director of Mariposa Investments, a company domiciled in the British Virgin Islands trying to establish a banking relationship with Dupont & Cie., the bank in Geneva that is also looking after the Montegrosso family's affairs. Samuel Jones will have had no problems opening accounts in many jurisdictions simply identifying himself as sole director of Mariposa Investments, no further questions asked. The provisions in the CDB however will require him to disclose to Dupont & Cie who the shareholders of Mariposa Investments are and if these shareholders are acting in a nominee capacity. The bank will have to probe deeper in order to satisfy the requirements of the CDB. Banks may not only ask for passport copies of the beneficial owners but also for further documentation explaining the nature of their relationship with the BVI company. Things will get even more complicated if Mariposa Investments is owned by a Trust. Let's say Mr. Jones tries to get away with disclosing that all of the voting shares of Mariposa Investments are owned by Veritas Trust, established under the BVI laws. Dupont & Cie will not be in compliance with the CDB by simply asking for passport copies of the trustees of Veritas Trust as is the case in many other jurisdictions. The bank will need to confirm the identity of the actual settlor, any protectors as well as any named beneficiaries. If there are no named beneficiaries, the trustees will have to sign a declaration to that effect and describe how trustees and protectors exercise their discretion over the trust assets. The elaborate framework of rules pertaining to the identification of account holders and whoever else has a beneficial interest in the account apply to those accounts that are identified by a number rather than a name as well. As we have examined earlier in the book, there are no anonymous accounts at Swiss banks.

Prohibition of active assistance in the flight of capital is another integral part of the CDB. Member banks for the

inside swiss banking

SBA are prohibited from providing assistance to their clients in transferring capital to Switzerland from countries that restrict the movement of capital outside of their jurisdiction. This is what happened in the Chiasso Affair when Credit Suisse executives helped Italian clients move assets across the Swiss-Italian border without complying with Italian regulations. The key word in this CDB clause is 'active' and the question of course is what type of action performed by a bank or their employees constitutes a prohibited 'active' assistance versus the purely 'passive' acceptance of moneys that have been exported to Switzerland illegally. As per the CDB's definition, accepting client moneys outside of Switzerland whereby a bank employee arranges for the capital to cross the border is a prohibited activity, as is the arrangement of so-called compensation deals. In these situations the bank would facilitate offsetting transactions between several of its clients in order to make the need redundant for money actually crossing the border and without clients knowing who their counterparties are. These types of transaction were part of the ordinary course of business for quite some time but are simply no longer viable in a banking environment that is built on full transparency of financial transactions. Lastly, banks are no longer allowed to actively work with unaffiliated firms or individuals that are in the business of arranging capital transfers from countries with exchange controls. This prohibition includes referring clients to these services. Back in the days of the Chiasso Affair, these cross-border traffickers had a good business going but with the referrals from Swiss banks stopping as a result of the CDB rules, the profession of 'cambisti' in Chiasso and other border towns in the South of Switzerland has seen its gold rush dwindle away. The image of a Swiss banker carrying a briefcase full of client cash across the border, however, is still very much alive even though this business practice has been outlawed by the CDB many years ago. I am a living example of this common misconception. I was in charge of the global private client business at one of the major Canadian banks and visiting the Bahamas and Cayman Islands for board meetings of our trust subsidiaries on the two islands in 2004. While there are direct flights between Toronto and Nassau and Grand Cayman separately, flying from Nassau to Cayman required me to stop in Miami. Within 24 hours I went through U.S. Immigrations at Miami International Airport twice, and I was travelling with a Swiss passport. This had to make Homeland Security suspicious. The second time through security, I was asked politely by an officer whether he could look through my carry-on bag and briefcase. I volunteered as I had nothing to hide. The two-day laundry, my toiletries and the Ludlum novel I carried with me were of limited interest to the officer and so were all the business papers in my briefcase. Then came the question: "If you don't mind me asking, Sir, where is the cash?" I showed him the couple

inside swiss banking

of tens and twenties as well as the handful of quarters in US and Canadian currency I carried in my pocket and asked whether this is what he wanted to see. His reply was that he wanted to see the 'real cash', the sort of cash usually carried in briefcases. After all I had declared that I was in charge of global private banking and that I was visiting the islands on business, so his expectation was to find significant amounts of cash crossing in and out of the United States. I tried to explain to the eager officer that this was not my modus operandi, that in fact I would fire any of my staff if it was brought to my attention that they were performing these kinds of services. This was simply not the kind of offshore business I or the bank I represented were engaged in. After a ten minute delay at the security desk, the officer handed me back my Swiss passport after he had entered a lengthy comment on his findings in the Homeland Security data base. I was allowed to continue my trip to Montreal where I had business meetings the next morning. The stuff that James Bond movies are made of still prevails in the imagination of law enforcement officers. I was worried that whatever the officer had entered into the database would create an inconvenient red flag on my future travels to the United States but I never got to find out because shortly after this incident, my family and I became Canadian citizens and we now travel on Canadian passports. Canadian bankers seem to be far less interesting or suspicious than those of the Swiss variety.

Lastly, the CDB contains provisions regarding the *'prohibition of active assistance in tax evasion and similar acts'*. As with the previous prohibition of assistance in the flight of capital, the key word here is 'active'. The CDB contains a rather narrow definition of what kinds of actions will be considered 'active assistance' with regards to tax matters, limiting the prohibited acts as those of providing incomplete or misleading attestations to either the client or to authorities in Switzerland or abroad. Putting it very simply, under the rules of the CDB a Swiss bank shall not lie for, and on behalf of, their clients by altering bank statements. This may seem to be nothing but common sense. Altering bank statements, trade confirms and similar documents would be illegal under any circumstance. The CDB just states the obvious and by doing so highlights the fact that more than one or two banks used to be in the business of supporting their clients' endeavours to make up stories by issuing incomplete, altered or otherwise misleading attestations. At the center of all such prohibited actions is a client's motive to deceive the recipient of the document and the bank's willingness to assist in the deception. Together with the objective to realize a gain of sorts, either personally or for someone else, deception is one of the critical elements defining fraud in the criminal sense. So you may ask why a prohibition to commit fraud or to conspire with a client committing fraud even had to be mentioned in the Code of Conduct. Let's use the

inside swiss banking

example of Samuel Jones, the sole director of Mariposa Investments again to make the point. Given the recent attention that the use of offshore vehicles in tax evasion schemes obtained in the U.S. Justice Department investigating the behaviour of UBS officials, one might think that tax schemes are the very essence of why someone would use an offshore vehicle to hold their assets. Nothing could be further from the truth. While it is indisputable that offshore structures are commonly used in connection with tax schemes, it would be inaccurate to conclude that those who use offshore companies and trusts to structure their wealth are by default evading tax in their home jurisdiction. If Samuel Jones asks his banker at Dupont & Cie to issue a confirmation that Mariposa Investments is the holder of account number 12345 but not to mention the other accounts held for the same company, he may simply reply to a request from someone doing business with Mariposa Investments that asks for a specific bank confirmation. The fact that additional accounts are wilfully omitted in the confirmation does not necessarily indicate that Samuel Jones is trying to hide material information from the recipient of the confirmation. However, Dupont & Cie will be well advised to inquire about the use of the requested confirmation in order to avoid becoming party to deceptive actions by Mariposa Investments. The bank will have to satisfy itself that there is a valid reason for their client to restrict the confirmation to a specific account only . If there is reason to believe that the client's objective is to mislead the recipient of the confirmation they will have to refuse providing the confirmation as requested. The banks have an obligation under the CDB to make sure that confirmations are not being used for deceptive purposes. This led to the established best practice that confirmations such as the one requested by Samuel Jones shall not be issued "To Whom it May Concern" but that the bank will insist in being given a real addressee before issuing the confirmation. This will allow the bank to determine whether its confirmation of only part of a business relationship is justified or not. If the confirmation is to be addressed to the Revenue Agency of the country in which the settlor of the trust owning the shares of Mariposa Investments is resident, there may be a problem. If on the other hand, the confirmation is intended for legal counsel of one of the beneficiaries of the trust and the account number referred to in the confirmation is the one in which the assets allocated to this beneficiary are being held, Mr Jones' request would be perfectly legitimate.

Sanctions: The CDB would not be worth much without the ability of the Swiss Bankers' Association (SBA) to enforce strict compliance with the due diligence and best practice rules contained in the CDB framework. The arsenal of sanctions that is available to the SBA reaches from reprimands in minor cases to fines of up to CHF 10 million that are levied from the bank responsible for the transgression. The level of the fines will usually depend on

inside swiss banking

the severity of the case as well as the capital base of the financial institution that had been charged. The sanctions are designed to hurt the financial institution and encourage behavioural change of the charged organization going forward. Large banks such as UBS and CS will therefore risk significantly higher fines for seemingly minor charges than a small regional bank. Violations of certain provisions of the CDB may also constitute offences under the Swiss Criminal Code such as the failure to properly identify counterparties of a banking transaction or assisting clients in money laundering activities. Detection of such illegal activity in CDB audits will in routinely lead to criminal charges against the individuals employed by the respective financial institution on top of any sanctions that are going to be imposed under the CDB framework.

All in all the CDB has proven to be a rather effective tool to police business behaviour at Swiss banks and to impose best practice throughout the system with a stiff framework of sanctions. This is of course not to say that bankers will not from time to time surrender to the temptation to engage in activities that are in violation of the CDB in order to feed their ambition, satisfy their greed, meet irrational performance goals or simply accommodate a persuasive client. We will explore this 'dark side' of Swiss private banking in the chapter that follows.

CHAPTER ELEVEN

Diamonds and Toothpaste

While the written policies, procedures and guidelines of financial institutions regulated by the Swiss Financial Markets Regulator demand strict compliance with the rules set out in the CDB and in Swiss Law, the reality of business practice sometimes looks quite different. Bankers are after all human and will from time to time make choices that are not in compliance with the framework of laws, rules and regulations. The motivation to break internal procedure or finance laws will of course be different by individual, situation or circumstance. Whether it is just good old greed, an attempt to meet budgets, the desire to please a client with unexpected service or the inability of an individual to deny a client a request that involves unlawful activity, certain bankers will find themselves compelled, from time to time, to make a bad choice. When assessing the risks they will conclude that, on balance, it is more likely than not that breaking the rules will advance their objectives and that they will, more likely than not, get away with it. In my past role as legal counsel of a major Swiss bank in the

inside swiss banking

1980s and 1990s, I had the opportunity to train a variety of private bankers, some rookies and some in senior roles, in legal matters. It always amazed me to see how people would calculate the risk of potentially getting caught in an unlawful act rather than accepting the fact that the legal and regulatory framework was changing and certain behaviours were no longer legally tenable. My students, junior and senior alike, often did not get to the logical conclusion on their own that their behaviour needed to change as a consequence of changes imposed in law. The ultimate service culture bred in the proverbial private banker an imperative to first please a client and ask for forgiveness later. It is a catch-me-if-you-can attitude that made many of them believe they were invincible in their quest for service excellence. This was a period of time in which new laws on insider trading, due diligence in financial matters and on the prevention of money laundering were introduced. It was the time when the banks' self regulation framework pulled in the reins on loose practices in an effort to clean up the damage caused by the involvement of certain Swiss banks with dubious clients, which further cast doubt on Switzerland as a reputable and reliable financial centre. And lastly, it was also a time in which the so far ubiquitous use of cash was replaced with wire transfers across institutions and across borders, making the movement of large sums of cash suspicious by default. Too much change for the typical private banker to deal with? Maybe, but hardly a good excuse to condone unlawful, risky and sometimes outright silly business practices.

In order to get a good measure of what constitutes acceptable business practice for a service-oriented private banker, one does not necessarily have to resort to exploring the line between what is legally permissible and what is not. Most of the time resorting to common sense will do but, as someone once said, common sense is the least common of all senses, and so it cannot always be counted on as the obvious yardstick. To use an example: it hardly makes good common sense for someone to carry hundreds of thousands of dollars in cash in a briefcase and transporting it in a car, train or airplane to a client's destination. So why is it then that private bankers of all stripes used to routinely provide this kind of transportation service until someone's briefcase got stolen? The answer could be quite simple: the bankers and their managers did not recognize the risks involved in the activity until it had materialized and generated a financial loss. In today's world the question is an entirely different one: Why would anyone run the risk of getting caught at the border with a briefcase full of cash or of having the same briefcase stolen at a gas station on the German autobahn while answering the call of nature? Considering that electronic wire transfers will safely move money from one account to another, between banks and across jurisdictions it seems that the need for carrying any more cash than that required

inside swiss banking

to pay for an espresso and a chocolate bar has been all but eliminated. Only those who want to avoid a paper trail or electronic record of a specific transaction will incur the risks of carrying large amounts of cash around. Large amounts of cash are unusual and raise suspicion regarding the motivation that drives both clients and their bankers to take such unnecessary risks. Bank clients that have nothing to hide don't have to take unnecessary risks. Those who feel the need to avoid a paper trail should not rely on their bankers assuming the risks for them. And lastly, bankers that do assist their clients in what presumably would be illegitimate objectives by taking inappropriate and unusual risks, expose themselves to sanctions under the various rules of the Criminal Code, financial regulation and bank policies.

The creativity applied in trying to hide the existence of illegitimate money does not stop at using cash. As the recent US Senate inquiry into the alleged conspiracy of certain UBS bankers with tax evading US clients shows, the imagination of clients and their banker alike can go haywire. The tighter the anticipated scrutiny of government officials, the sillier the manoeuvres tend to become. No-one will be able to rationally explain why Bradley Birkenfeld, a senior banker in the employ of UBS, a leading global wealth management firm would choose to hide diamonds in a tube of toothpaste contained in their personal toiletry case. Our self professed secret agent must have thought this had to be one of the safest ways to go undetected when transporting client assets into the US. He probably took pride in making the assumption that diamonds are sparkly in daylight but couldn't be detected by security screens. The fact that Birkenfeld was successful in smuggling the sparkly gems across the US border was sheer luck. If a Homeland Security officer would have chosen to check his bag, the smuggled diamonds would have found their way out of the toothpaste into confiscation and Birkenfeld would have gotten a ticket to jail. It may have seemed like a good idea at the time when our banker and his client decided to combine diamonds and toothpaste for a successful smuggle through US Customs and Immigration. However, when Birkenfeld decided to recant his James Bond-like activities to law enforcement in the US in the context of the US tax case against UBS (see Chapter 15), the scheme created a nightmare for UBS. As "Mr. Smart's" employer, the world's leading wealth management firm had a lot of explaining to do.

There was never any doubt that UBS's code of conduct and related policies unequivocally outlawed this kind of behaviour. However, the fact that this kind of spy novel behaviour was demonstrated by a UBS employee to whom important client relationships had been entrusted, naturally reflected badly on the firm's institutional judgement. No matter what was written in the policies, the question had to be asked whether this type of action was

inside swiss banking

condoned by management. And more importantly the question was raised as to what kind of moral compass a firm could possibly have, that employed banking professionals who showed this kind of contempt for laws and policies, and who lacked the common sense to realize that using toothpaste to make client assets invisible was not that brilliant an idea in the first place.

The lessons to be learned from this incident are many. For one it shows how little hesitation certain individuals will have to make complete fools of themselves in their desire to please clients with illegitimate requests. It also demonstrates that written policies and guidelines are useless if the organization issuing them does not make sure compliance with them is enforced at all times. If this is not done, the firm will look like an organization that condones, directly or tacitly, the type of catch-me-if-you-can philosophy that apparently still exists in the heads of certain bankers. Lastly, and perhaps most importantly, it demonstrates how difficult it is for an institution like UBS to defend its policy and governance framework when the idiocy of a few of its employees is broadcast to the world. Through the US Senate investigation, the story of diamonds and toothpaste became the smoking gun of Swiss bankers acting like members of a spy agency rather than employees of a reputable bank. Nobody will be surprised to read that this translated into one of the most significant reputational issues any bank could possibly face. UBS paid dearly for the cavalier attitude employed by their senior management in dealing with the many issues relating to offshore banking. In the public eye, UBS was accused of having lost a sense of ethics and morality 'tout simple'. The organization's loss of dozens of billions in client assets in 2008 and 2009 can be directly attributed to the reputational damage that the bank suffered from their problems with the US authorities and the question marks they brought to light regarding UBS's moral and ethical compass. But the nightmare did not stop with the exodus of clients. Employees in New York and London, Toronto and Hong Kong started to ask themselves whether working for this kind of organization was something they could afford to be seen doing. Within only a few weeks, employees across the globe replaced their pride of association with the UBS brand with the concern of how they could explain to family and friends that they worked there.

As UBS continues to lick its wounds from the hit taken in the US, the increased scrutiny of offshore banking that came with their problems has severely impacted the private banking industry, not only in Switzerland but in other jurisdictions such as Luxembourg, Monaco or Singapore as well. As we will explore in more detail later, the aggressive stance taken vis-à-vis UBS by the US Department of Justice (DOJ) and the IRS had an unprecedented ripple effect into Europe and Asia, leading to a global overhaul of international cooperation in tax

inside swiss banking

matters. It is hardly a surprise that the global financial and fiscal crisis brought revenue ministries across the globe out of hibernation as governments try to fill gaps in their treasuries. The OECD and the G10 have increased the pressure on traditional offshore centres to show more cooperation in the fight against tax offences of all levels. Some say that people like the inventive UBS banker, with the brilliant idea of hiding diamonds in his tube of toothpaste, are to be blamed for the flurry of political activity that has recently been developed on this topic. While there may be some truth in this, it is probably more accurate to say that the days of traditional offshore banking, where the main objective was to hide assets, have long been numbered and that this era of international banking is now coming to an end. This process may well have been accelerated by the global financial crisis and the fact that governments are engaged in an ever-increasing framework of international co-operation. Untenable business practices are just that; they cannot be sustained and banks with a significant exposure to the offshore market will have to rapidly adjust to the change that is imminent. This is true for Swiss banks of course as they are the most prominent participants in the global offshore market, but it applies to the many other jurisdictions just the same. As far as Switzerland is concerned, the events surrounding the US troubles of UBS have demonstrated very harshly the vulnerabilities of a financial centre whose success largely depends on doing business with international wealth. Over the last one hundred years, neutral Switzerland has built a reputation as a safe haven for assets that attracted billions of dollars in private wealth. The proverbial bank secrecy and confidentiality served as the main competitive advantage of Switzerland over other jurisdictions. Assets gathered in Switzerland through global private banking support the whole banking sector and thus are of critical importance for the sustainability of Zurich as major global financial centre. As the global fiscal environment enters into a new era and Switzerland decides to show more international cooperation in tax matters, an important part of the historic value proposition of Swiss banks evaporates. Yvan Pictet, Senior Partner at Pictet & Cie, estimated in a media interview shortly after the Swiss Government decided to release the names of a few hundred US clients of UBS to the IRS, that Swiss private banks such as Pictet stand to lose close to half of their traditional business under a scenario in which Switzerland abolishes its unique distinction of tax evasion and tax fraud, the topic of the next chapter. In order to survive in a rapidly changing financial and fiscal environment, Swiss banks not only have to stop engaging in diamond-and-toothpaste types of operations on behalf of their clients; they have to reinvent their global value proposition altogether.

inside swiss banking

CHAPTER TWELVE

Tax Evasion, Fraud and Amnesties

As we have examined earlier, the issue of tax is inextricably linked to the topic of Swiss private banking in the minds of many. Whenever the concept of keeping assets in Zurich, Geneva or Lugano comes up for discussion, so does the conclusion that whoever keeps their money with a bank in Switzerland probably cheats on the tax man in their home country. The notion of Switzerland as a tax haven is engrained in the common mind across the globe, even though there is nothing in the Swiss tax code that would support the idea. With an average marginal income tax rate in the forty percent range Switzerland's tax regime is well within global averages and contrary to the U.S. or Canada, the Swiss also tax the accumulation of wealth with a hefty asset tax. While capital gains taxation has been abolished in most Swiss tax jurisdictions, several years ago there was increasing pressure to reintroduce taxation of proceeds from investments during the bull market of the early years of the new millennium. The years ahead may well see these efforts come to fruition in the

105

fight against the effects that the financial market crisis and the ensuing recession have on the overall tax base. Just like other jurisdictions Switzerland imposes a withholding tax on income earned in local currency regardless of an investor's domicile. In addition there are a number of other levies and duties that are payable in Switzerland whether someone is registered as a tax payer there or not, such as the stamp duties levied on new issues and on trades made on the Swiss stock exchange. And to round things out, Switzerland collects a tax on the sale of goods and services like most countries do. Looking at it this way, Switzerland is no more a tax haven than any of the G10 countries. For example, a Mexican resident can open a bank account in Canada or Switzerland and avoid being taxed on income from investments held in the account in either country as long as they avoid collecting income in Canadian Dollars or Swiss Francs. The same client may actually experience a lower level of overall taxation on their investments in Canada due to the absence of stamp duties and other levies that are payable to the Swiss but not to the Canadian Revenue Agency. On the other hand, holding assets in Toronto or Zurich does not relieve the client to report the income collected in their Mexican tax return as Mexico, like most other nations, imposes tax to its residents on worldwide income. What is it then that created the notion that most foreign clients doing business with Swiss banks will do so for tax reasons? The answer does not necessarily

inside swiss banking

lie in the level and types of taxation under Swiss law but in the basic principles governing the tax system.

Switzerland's tax system relies on the principle of self declaration and on the general notion that the level of taxation imposed on a resident should be reasonable so that overall Swiss tax payers will show a high degree of tax honesty. The government enforces its tax laws on an individual basis. Anchored in the principle that someone's financial affairs are covered by an individual's right to privacy from the government, there is no automated exchange of financial data between financial institutions and tax authorities as known across the European Union or North America. As far as tax delinquency is concerned, Swiss tax codes make a distinction between criminal and non-criminal offences. While tax offences committed by way of fraudulent activity are punishable as tax fraud under the Criminal Code, offences that simply involve incomplete disclosures made on a tax return are characterized as tax evasion and will result in fines imposed under the tax code without criminal prosecution. This distinction between criminally punishable tax fraud and simple tax evasion makes the Swiss tax system unique. Together with the lack of a central government database on income earned from investments, it is the main factor that has led to Switzerland becoming the destination of choice for those international clients that wish to escape the grip of their country's revenue agencies. Keeping assets in Switzerland obviously does not relieve them from the duty to declare the generated income in their home country tax return. However, failure to do so would be virtually risk free as long as it did not constitute fraud under Swiss law. Only if a case could be made by their home country tax agency that the acts of the investor represent common fraud would the Swiss provide legal assistance in a foreign-based criminal investigation. The distinction in the Swiss tax system of tax fraud and tax evasion would play out in favour of all those foreign clients that simply tried to keep a nest egg inaccessible to the tax agency of their home country. Since the Swiss do not police their tax payers by way of automated data flows between financial institutions and the Government within Switzerland they certainly have no reason to extend this courtesy to tax authorities outside. This has created an environment of relative safety for those who chose Switzerland to stash away a rainy day fund while by and large complying with the tax laws of their home jurisdictions. As long as the reported income in their home country remained inconspicuous they had little to fear in terms of tax authorities raising suspicion and starting to investigate their financial situation. Problems would only arise if the money kept offshore was used to fund a lifestyle that exceeded the realm of plausibility when compared with the assets and income declared in tax returns. We will get to this topic a little later.

inside swiss banking

International clients have taken advantage of the subtle differences in the Swiss tax system for decades. It is impossible to assess how many of the billions worth of foreign assets booked in Switzerland never found their way on to a domestic tax return; nobody keeps a statistic on the rate at which Swiss bank clients evade taxes in their home country. However, it is safe to assume that governments around the globe have known for decades about the practice of a certain percentage of tax payers not complying with their domestic tax obligations and moving assets offshore beyond the reach of authorities. Tax departments from Washington to Paris, from London to Berlin and Rome knew what was going on but until recently the problem of losing tax dollars due to tax evasion was simply not significant enough to create a big stir. Dealing with the phenomenon of international tax evasion has its complexities as it touches on the fundamentals of state sovereignty, presumed innocence and probable cause as well as the world of diplomacy with its game of give-and-take. In addition, tax evasion is an issue that touches not only Switzerland, a small neutral country with some diplomatic clout, but a wide range of offshore banking centres, some of them located in the distant waters of the South Pacific (Vanuatu or Nauru), other members of the European Union (Luxembourg, Austria and Liechtenstein) and some subjects of the British Sovereign (Channel Islands, Cayman, BVI). As can easily be imagined from the diversity of this list of countries, offshore finance is an area in which double standards go rampant, creating a political hot potato that is best left untouched as long as things don't get out of control. When dealing with the issue of offshore finance, one could not single out Switzerland without exposing Jersey or Luxembourg, which might open a Pandora's Box within the European Union. In contrast, the smaller offshore jurisdictions in the Caribbean and the South Pacific were much easier to pin down and put on a black list. As a result, organizations like the OECD have for decades focused their effort of curbing the movement of assets offshore to the small jurisdictions that have typically been associated with shady business and facilitating money laundering. Based on the pressure that the practice of blacklisting has put on these jurisdictions, an effort has been made by the vast majority of them to catch up with FATF standards and assist in the global fight against money laundering and terrorist financing. In the aftermath of 9-11 this was a much higher priority than pushing the agenda on global cooperation in tax matters.

In recent months the U.S. DOJ and the IRS have somehow taken the reins in the global fight against tax evasion. Using the legal clout at the United States' disposal, they forced one of the global leaders in wealth management to cooperate with a series of U.S. tax probes or face the prospect of being declared a criminal organization under U.S. statutes. Those that have followed the Enron case

inside swiss banking

know that the U.S. government slapping this label on a large corporation will almost certainly lead to its demise in bankruptcy. Priorities have changed and the United States have raised the bar. Other countries have taken a different approach to increasing tax compliance. They don't attack the banks that their tax payers have been using to hide assets but rather create the incentive of tax amnesties to convince delinquent tax payers to come clean. One reason why countries like Italy have chosen this path may lie in the fact that their legal system does not arm them with the same kind of prosecutorial powers as exist in the U.S. Another reason may be the natural reluctance of nation states to depend on coordinated international action when dealing with a sovereign issue such as taxes. It is much easier to deal with tax on your own than to try and convince all members of an international organization such as the European Union or the OECD to agree on a common policy on tax delinquency. Lastly, tax amnesties deal with reality: Every parent knows that it is more effective to use incentives to cause desired behaviours than it is to raise the bar on sanctions. Not that tax avoiders should be compared to misbehaving children but the past success of amnesty programs speaks for itself. In the early 1990s the Italian Government declared a tax amnesty for any Italian tax payer that voluntarily disclosed assets held offshore. The program was designed to repatriate funds held mainly in Switzerland and Monaco and to reintegrate the assets in the Italian economy. Delinquent tax payers that participated in the amnesty were spared tax penalties and criminal sanctions and got away with paying overdue taxes for only a few years thus preserving most of the assets. Billions of dollars found their way back into the Italian banking system as a result, not to mention the field day that lawyers and accountants had in dealing with clients that wanted to take this opportunity to come clean without prohibitive penalties and fines. The incentive program worked on all counts.

The Italian amnesty program was so much a success that it had some larger Swiss banks rethink their business strategy in dealing with international clients. The success of the amnesty brought the intrinsic vulnerability of offshore banking to the surface: What will happen if all of a sudden international clients no longer see a benefit in dealing with bankers in traditional offshore centres? Banks with large client clusters in certain countries that might follow Italy's lead were faced with the prospect that a good number of their clients might take advantage of the amnesty benefits and repatriate their money. Repatriated assets would be lost forever as the terms of the amnesty typically required the assets to remain with a local financial institution. In order to counter this risk to their asset base, Swiss banks started to develop an international 'onshore' strategy. Under this new strategy banks like UBS were opening branches and subsidiaries to gain access to the

inside swiss banking

onshore banking and wealth management business in major markets across Europe. The idea was that building an onshore business in key markets like France, Germany, Spain, Italy and Great Britain would enable the bank to keep assets if they ever were to be repatriated, be it under a new tax amnesty or as a result of voluntary disclosures made by clients to their home country tax agencies. The new focus on onshore opportunities outside of Switzerland led to a flurry of acquisitions in key markets in an effort of the banks to get faster traction in their European expansion. Banks like UBS acquired boutique wealth managers wherever an opportunity for a strategic fit presented itself and used them as a platform from which to rapidly increase the footprint. International clients now had a choice of dealing with the same Swiss bank either locally or in Switzerland or even both. The future will show whether this 'onshoring' of international private banking will be successful. So far most of the banks that have embarked on an aggressive expansion strategy will have to admit that their onshore businesses barely break even while the old-style offshore business conducted out of Switzerland continues to generate handsome profits. Even after a decade, the costs of acquiring the boutique businesses combined with the costs of hiring additional bankers and integrating business platforms are still eating into the profitability of the onshore strategy. In an environment of reduced revenues due to the market crisis of 2008 and 2009 this will likely lead to various Swiss institutions reconsidering the viability of their expanded global presence. Some of them are prone to get out of markets just as the next wave of tax driven repatriations starts.

A debate has recently started across the globe about the reliability of Switzerland as a confidential custodian of assets in the aftermath of the U.S. tax inquiries against UBS and the Swiss Financial Market Regulator ordering the release of select client data to the IRS to safeguard national interest. It is not unreasonable to think that this debate may have a number of traditional offshore clients rethink their loyalty to Swiss banks and to Switzerland as a place to hold assets in. Those with a clean tax record may simply not want to be associated with the heightened scrutiny that the existence of an offshore account in Zurich may bring. Those with a tax issue to contend with may fear that their home country authorities are coming after them in which case they need to beat them in a race against the clock. Voluntary disclosure benefits only accrue to those who declare before the tax agency has caught up with them. In both cases the rate of repatriation of assets increases and those banks that have withdrawn from onshore markets or have failed to build a sufficiently stable domestic business will miss the chance to become an active part of the repatriation effort.

inside swiss banking

CHAPTER THIRTEEN

Swiss Accounts and French Châteaux

In my role as legal counsel for a major Swiss bank in the early nineties, I came across a French client whose official tax residence was in Montreux on the beautiful north shore of Lake Geneva. The Swiss Canton of Vaud, in which Montreux is located, offers foreigners a tax deal in which they can get the benefit of full tax residence for a flat tax based on only a fraction of their wealth. This attracted a variety of wealthy celebrities to the shores of Lake Geneva, including Jackie Stewart, Michael Schumacher and Shania Twain. The French client was not a celebrity like them; but he was a Count with significant wealth which was managed through a number of offshore foundations and trusts. His two children were French citizens residing in France. The daughter was a housewife married to a government bureaucrat while the son was a doctor working at a hospital in a small town in Burgundy. None of them had any source of wealth and led a lifestyle that seemed unacceptable to their father with the nice view on the mountains of Savoy. The irony was that he lived in

115

Switzerland while the view from his hillside apartment was across the lake into France where his children lived within much more modest means. He had followed their success in school when they all lived in their French castle. Both children graduated with honours from major universities yet in his view they could not seem to get anywhere with their lives. Maybe it was parental guilt that drove his desire to help; in any event the thought that his children were not able to afford their own 'château' in the French country was unbearable to him. His foundation and trust held various millions and he was intent on finding a way to fund his children's quest for a better future now that they needed it most. The Count's problem was that when he had left France a couple of decades earlier, his tax returns seemed to suggest that he was navigating close to poverty. The offshore assets he had accumulated over decades had never been disclosed to the French fiscal authorities. As far as the official record went, he was a man with average means. Helping his children with the purchase of a country estate involved assets nobody knew about. He was about to make a donation to his children through an anonymous vehicle sitting in Liechtenstein with money coming from a bank in Switzerland to fund a real estate transaction in France that was going to be a matter of public record. The count was surprised to learn that there was no way he was going to use the money he had so meticulously accumulated offshore to help his children in France without the risk that the decade-

inside swiss banking

old manoeuvres to evade the French revenue department would eventually come to light. Financing a real estate purchase with undeclared offshore assets was almost certainly going to lead to the purchasers being questioned about the source of the sudden windfall of wealth. According to the childrens' tax returns, the purchase of a country estate was well beyond their means and they seemed to come from a family with modest resources. Of course the French children could simply answer that they received a donation from an offshore trust but the questioning would not stop there. The French fiscal police was known for their relentlessness. They would be going to put pressure on the beneficiaries to provide satisfactory answers or to get them from third parties. It was only a matter of time before they would get to the father in Switzerland, most likely not on Swiss territory as the Swiss would not tolerate activity by a foreign agency on their soil, but when he next set foot into France. This was not a risk that the count was willing to take. He needed to be able to travel freely between Switzerland and France to see his children and grandchildren. Maybe there were alternative ways? His children could get financing from a French bank and the count's bank in Switzerland could back the mortgage with guarantees and even make the mortgage payments. Of course this was not a viable shortcut either as the French bank would have to ask the same questions to satisfy their obligations under know-your-client rules and other compliance regulations. Maybe the Swiss bank could find a way to issue a letter of credit in their own name to secure the French loan; in this case nobody had to know the ultimate provider of the funds. This too, was not a viable solution. It would constitute indirect conspiracy of the Swiss bank to mislead a third party to perpetuate an act of tax evasion. Such level of accommodation of the count's desires would violate the CDB.

I have used the example of the French count to demonstrate the limited use of undeclared assets held in offshore bank accounts. To many, the accumulation of rainy day money away from the grip of tax authorities seems like a good idea when faced with what they see as prohibitively high taxation. Many states within the E.U. have their calendar mark for "tax free" day well into July. An overall tax burden above fifty percent is generally viewed the kind of threshold past which tax payer mutiny starts to kick in. This drives the rate of tax delinquency up and in some countries makes tax evasion something like a national sport for the wealthy. While risky, moving assets out of the country of residence into an offshore account in Switzerland, Cayman or Singapore is the easy part. This is why many of those who play the sport become too greedy or even addicted to the thrill. They accumulate wealth offshore while keeping visible earnings in their home countries to a bare minimum. The real problem facing these types of bank clients does not lie in getting the assets

inside swiss banking

offshore. It starts when they try to use the offshore wealth to fund a lifestyle that in the eyes of the tax inspectors is beyond their means. What is money worth if you can't use it? How much is enough to create a rainy day fund to support the family in an emergency? And how much fun is it to be rich if you can't live the life of the wealthy? Once clients ask themselves these questions they will come to realize that by accumulating significant wealth outside of their "official" life they have created a significant problem rather than an opportunity to lead a carefree lifestyle. They become prisoners of their own greed. They have seemingly beaten the system but at significant cost. As they ponder what to do with the money stashed away they find that the peace of mind they wanted to create continues to elude them. My experience over many years of dealing with these kinds of situations has constantly been that tax evasion is hardly a strategy for the long term. To use space travel as an analogy: People can find a way to fly to the moon but if they have not figured out how to get back, there is a problem. While the moving of assets offshore is often planned meticulously, more often than not people will improvise when spending the money. As long as the money does not track back into the original jurisdiction this usually does not create an issue. Secret stashes may be fine to pay for a month-long cruise on a private yacht in the Aegean Sea or even for a Miro painting purchased at a Sotheby's auction, as long it is kept in an offshore bank vault and not displayed at home. However, it is close to impossible to access these same stashes to bail out the account owner's illiquid manufacturing business in their home country. No matter what the subtle differences made by Swiss tax laws on evasion and fraud, proceeds of tax evasion have the same legal property as any proceeds of unlawful activity. The real difficulty lies in their re-integration in legitimate flows of money.

Our French count may decide that helping his children with the purchase of a 'petit château' in the French country may not be worth the fiscal risks and keep his trusts and foundations untouched. Once he passes away dealing with the assets held in Lausanne will be his children's problem. They are the beneficiaries and will have to find a way to use the assets by themselves when the time comes. Once the French siblings get the phone call from the offshore trustees informing them about the sudden windfall of wealth, the nice surprise may soon start to feel like a bad dream. How come their father had stashed away all this money and never helped them when they needed his assistance the most? The estate's lawyers will explain to them that they basically have two options: Option One is to leave the assets where they are and just use the funds to pay for vacations and other inconspicuous expenses while the bulk of the capital is left untouched. Option Two is to voluntarily disclose their beneficiary status to the French authorities. This will allow them to use the assets to fund projects in their home country, such as purchasing the country estate they always wanted or funding a medical practice. The choice they both need to make is whether they want to have the assets available to them in their entirety, in which case they would have to pay back taxes and penalties, or to leave the tax status of the assets alone, in which case they have only limited use of the new-found wealth. The divergence of choices to be made can lead to an interesting debate between the two siblings. Imagine the brother working as a physician in a regional hospital. He may decide that he would have good use for his portion to start his own medical clinic. The sister on the other hand is quite content with her current lifestyle based on the stable salary and prospects for a good pension that marriage to a public servant comes with. She has no burning interest in a voluntary disclosure while her brother won't be able to realize his dream without it. However, the two are in this together. A voluntary disclosure made by one of them will put the other under pressure to do the same or to face uncomfortable questions from the revenue department. It won't take them too long to become suspicious. Likewise, even if both siblings agree on not disclosing, a silly mistake committed by one of them in the future may put the other one in jeopardy.

The lesson to be learned from this analysis is that simple tax evasion as committed by our French count may work for the first generation involved, as long as nobody needs to access the funds. For the second generation it is a whole different story. They likely will want to use the money and not keep growing it secretly. They won't really have a choice but to come clean, preferably under treatment as voluntary disclosure. A good portion of the accumulated wealth will go to the treasury department but at least what is left will be accessible and nobody has to live in fear of being found out.

inside swiss banking

CHAPTER FOURTEEN

National Sovereignty

in a Cross Border Business

The international legal system generally accepts the principle that all nation states have the right to establish their own rule of law under full sovereignty. It also acknowledges the right of nation states to protect themselves against attacks from other jurisdictions on their sovereignty. However, the growing international cooperation of nation states under frameworks such as the United Nations, Free Trade Agreements, the G10 or even the Guidelines of the European Union has led to a significant degree of dilution of sovereign rule. The international community exercises a high degree of political and legal pressure on its members to agree on principles of cooperation in matters of international interest such as security and defence, human rights, trade, energy and environmental sustainability. While taxation used to be one of the last realms of national sovereignty, efforts to create a commonly accepted framework of international tax rules

123

have recently been stepped up by the G10, the EU and the OECD. National sovereignty is much more narrowly defined today than ever since the creation of the concept of sovereign nation states. In a globalized economy there is much less room for major market participants having differing views on key issues affecting the free and fair movement of goods, services and people. Allowing individual nation states to veer too far off from a commonly accepted standard in a global marketplace will create distortions and disadvantages for others. In order to ensure that an integrated market works fairly and properly there needs to be a reasonably level playing field for all participants. This in turn requires individual nation states to put their self-interest behind the collective interest of the global community.

Switzerland is a small country in the middle of Europe, surrounded by nation states that are organized under the banner of the European Union. For centuries the Swiss Confederation withstood pressure to submit to the rules of powerful neighbours. The definition of Neutrality as the basic principle of Swiss foreign policy has allowed Switzerland to stay out of two World Wars and establish itself as a reliable partner in international diplomacy. For decades the principle of Neutrality has proven its diplomatic usefulness, not only for the Swiss but for the global community. It gave Switzerland the aura of an indispensable nation in an increasingly complex global

inside swiss banking

community. Geneva became one of the most prominent locations not only for private banking but also for high-stakes diplomatic conferences. Agreements were signed there on the restoration of peace in Indochina (1954), on nuclear weapons testing (1958), on the Arab-Israeli conflict (1973) and the peace process between Israel and Palestine in 2003. Most recently, Geneva was chosen as the venue for a high-power and high-stakes conference on how to deal with Iran's nuclear ambitions. When diplomatic relations between Iran and the United States of America were discontinued in the aftermath of the US hostage crisis in the early 1980s, the Swiss Government was chosen as the logical interlocutor between the two nations. As we will discuss in the next chapter, the indispensable role of Switzerland in diplomacy between the US and Iran may well have played a role in the resolution of the United States' most recent effort to impose its legal framework against Swiss banks, most notably UBS. However, as the Swiss learned in the Holocaust debate in the late 1990s, diplomatic good services are of limited use in business. They cannot be depended upon as a bargaining chip when it comes to defending Swiss sovereignty in a globalized economy. The case of the IRS and the Justice Department vs. UBS is no different. Besides its neutrality Switzerland has little to offer that would give it legal or political clout in the global community. After all it is just a spot on the map, a country of 7 million people without natural resources and

125

a domestic economy that would hardly be able to provide jobs and food to all of its residents. Switzerland is not part of the G8, the G10 or even the recently formalized G20 club of the most relevant nations. It has only recently joined the United Nations even though Geneva has hosted UN conferences and UN agencies such as the WHO from the time they were created. Over the decades following World War II the Swiss have built a reputation of a nation that will use its neutral status to limit its cooperation in global affairs to those areas that benefit Swiss national interest. The Swiss had to learn, however, that the world's increasing and accelerated integration economically as well as politically limits the usefulness of the Helvetic Confederation's neutral status. The recent attacks on Swiss sovereignty in tax matters are a prime example of this development.

In order to sustain their economy the Swiss depend heavily on the export of goods and services and on the success of the multi-national corporations that are headquartered there. The Swiss economy has benefited for decades from the transfer of prosperity that occurs as a result of the multi-national activity of some of its largest companies such as pharmaceutical giants Novartis and Roche, engineering firms Sulzer and ABB, food conglomerate Nestlé, and of course the globally active banking sector. It should come as no surprise that this transfer of wealth from the European Union, the US and other nations into Switzerland creates demands regarding

inside swiss banking

generally accepted sovereign behaviour. A country whose very sustainability depends on its participation in the global marketplace cannot pretend to be an island that need not bother with the perceptions of its trading partners. Whether the Swiss like it or not they have to accept the fact that globalization of trade and the world's economy leads to increasing pressure for Switzerland to evolve as a sovereign nation. Switzerland will have to adopt changes to its legal system to make it more compatible with international standards.

Multi-national corporations like globally active banks understand how national laws in different markets will affect their business, regardless of what the Swiss rules and regulations state. Business conducted in jurisdictions outside of Switzerland falls under the purview of the legal frameworks of said jurisdiction. Contrary to what some Swiss bankers may wish to believe the secrecy provisions contained in the Swiss Bank Act will not protect them when traveling abroad. As soon as an individual in the employ of a Swiss-based banking institution sets foot across the border into a foreign country, the rules of that country will apply to whatever it is the employee is doing there. If they get caught speeding on one of the few stretches of the German Autobahn with a speed limit, they will expect to be fined under the German traffic laws. The same applies to them being interrogated by a border control officer if they get caught with a briefcase full of client statements. Any attempt to invoke Swiss bank secrecy to avoid answering questions will be met with disbelief first and followed up by legal sanctions to provide truthful answers. As they expanded their business activities beyond the Swiss borders, global Swiss banks have learned in past decades that their business practices need to comply with the laws and regulations in any jurisdiction they are active in, regardless of what changes the Swiss government has made or will be making to Swiss law as international political pressure increases. UBS, the most prominent of the Swiss global banks has recently made an experience they wish they never had to make, on how significant the impact of non-compliance with US law can be on their home market activities. We will explore details of this in the next chapter.

As we have discussed earlier in this chapter, some foreign governments and their agencies are less than enchanted with the international legal assistance process offered by their Swiss counterparts. Access to banking information on suspected tax cheats is difficult to obtain. It usually requires enforcement agencies to build a case against a suspect in their home country based on sketchy evidence as most of it resides in Switzerland. The image of the tail wagging the dog comes to mind: In order to get the Swiss authorities to grant a request for legal assistance, a foreign tax enforcement agency will have to provide sufficient evidence that a suspected tax cheat has committed a qualified tax offence. This evidence would typically include

inside swiss banking

the very bank records that are the object of the legal assistance request. No bank records, no sufficient proof for legal assistance. No bank records from Switzerland, no case in the jurisdiction that requests the information. No wonder that certain tax authorities in countries bordering with Switzerland grew increasingly frustrated.

This frustration gave rise to foreign government agencies developing creative new ways to obtain the information that eluded them. Over the past decades there have been several cases in which law enforcement agents of neighbouring countries tried to obtain vital banking information on some of their citizens directly in Switzerland. These undercover operations usually unfolded like this: A plainclothes agent would follow their fellow citizens across the border to their banking destination in Switzerland, mostly in border towns such as Basel, Geneva or Lugano. They would take pictures as the objects of surveillance entered the bank building and wait inconspicuously for them to exit the building again. If the tagged citizen was accompanied by a third party such as their bank manager who was taking them to lunch, pictures would be taken of this person as well. On rare occasions not only the client but also the banker would be tagged on their way home so that the undercover agent could ascertain their identity. Some undercover agents would even pose as prospective clients and arrange to meet with the tagged bankers on false pretence to complete their intelligence. They would ask all sorts of questions regarding banking services in general and particularly with respect to the exchange of information with foreign tax authorities and what precautions existed to prevent unwanted access to bank records. Not only did these practices violate international law enforcement protocol, they constituted illegal gathering of intelligence on foreign soil under the Swiss Criminal Code. Regardless they occurred on a regular basis until some of the less cautious foreign agents got caught in the act and apprehended by Swiss authorities. The motivation of the French, Italian or German agents to break Swiss law was much deeper than sheer curiosity; they were sent on a mission to nail alleged tax offenders and to build undeniable evidence against them. Breaking Swiss law on Swiss soil was part of the mission and a commonly accepted risk. High stakes operations always cause collateral damage. However, the fact that some of them were caught in engaging in illegal activities led to significant diplomatic disturbance. The practice was discontinued once head quarters in Paris, Berlin or Rome lost the defence of plausible deniability. After all the system of global assistance among international law enforcement depends on some level of etiquette and mutually agreed rules of engagement. As we have discussed in previous chapters, Switzerland makes its law enforcement system available to foreign prosecutors through a generally accessible international legal assistance framework. Foreign nations that engage in

inside swiss banking

illegal gathering of evidence on Swiss soil outside of the established laws and treaties run the risk that any request for legal assistance might be met with red tape rather than a sentiment of cooperation. In severe cases the Swiss might even consider not providing legal assistance to a foreign nation showing contempt for Swiss sovereignty.

With Swiss banks controlling the largest share of offshore assets held by high net worth individuals globally it is no surprise that Switzerland's privacy and bank secrecy laws find few supporters in the global political arena. As we have examined, attacks on Switzerland's sovereignty are not a specifically recent phenomenon. What has changed in recent years is the intensity with which they are being carried out. Undercover activity by foreign tax agents has been replaced by concerted action on the political stage. The European Union and the United States have opened a unified front against Switzerland as a tax haven. Mounting international pressure culminated with the Swiss government agreeing in March 2009 to negotiate new tax treaties with all its major trading partners. The objective is to find a framework in which to provide legal assistance to foreign tax agencies not only in cases of tax fraud but in cases of simple tax evasion as well. The US Senate investigation of UBS and the related legal action by the DOJ and the IRS have been a major catalyst in this chain of events. Let us explore what happened.

CHAPTER FIFTEEN

The US Attacks on UBS

Switzerland and the US have a friendly relationship that goes almost back to the Declaration of Independence. The two "Sister Republics", as they are often called, share similar democratic values. The early US have been inspired by the concept of Federalism established by the 13 original states of the Swiss Confederation and Switzerland took inspiration from the American Constitution when it formed the world's second federal state in 1848. During the Civil War Ferdinand Buchser, a Swiss artist was commissioned to paint portraits of the opposing Generals Sherman and Lee. Both portraits currently hang side-by-side in the Swiss Embassy in Washington, a historic curiosity to illustrate the bond between the two nations of disproportionate size and importance. Swiss banks have been active in the US longer than in most other foreign jurisdictions, except the UK. Swiss Bank Corporation, now part of UBS, was the first Swiss bank to open a presence in New York in 1939. Swiss banks established themselves in the US before most of their European competitors and both UBS and Credit Suisse

inside swiss banking

today are major players in US capital markets. The Swiss have long admired the United States concept of freedom and opportunity and for the internationally active Swiss banks establishing a presence in the US was a no-brainer. Not only was this the land of opportunity, it also happened to be the single most important financial power as the world emerged from two world wars. Banks like Swiss Bank Corporation, Union Bank of Switzerland and Credit Suisse, all with global ambition, simply had to be there. The seemingly unlimited opportunities would reward them for the risk of entering an unknown market across the Atlantic, especially as early entrants. Conversely, not being a market player in the United States would put any global Swiss bank at a significant disadvantage vis-à -vis other global financial institutions. This was certainly the case for investment banking which is why Swiss banks became very active in finding ways to improve their access to US capital markets in the last couple of decades of the Twentieth Century. Credit Suisse made a landmark acquisition with First Boston while several years later Swiss Bank Corporation found partners in O'Connor Associates, Brinson Partners and Dillon Read. Even with these acquisitions, Swiss banks' reach into the US market was limited to the wholesale part of the business. This was true until the year 2000 when UBS acquired Paine Webber, the country's fifth largest retail brokerage firm. Founded in Boston in 1880, the 120 year-old Painer Webber was one of the best known and most venerable brands in America. With a transaction value of over ten billion dollars this acquisition of one of the pre-eminent U.S. stock brokerages truly was a big deal. Not only was it by far the largest transaction involving a foreign bank on U.S. soil, dwarfing any acquisition that a foreign bank had made in the U.S. before; more importantly an icon in the American wealth management landscape had fallen into foreign hands. This was new territory for the Swiss and the Americans alike. Acquiring Paine Webber was a true game changer as it transformed the nature of the relationship that Swiss banks had with the US market. Before 2000, Swiss banks, along with their foreign bank peers, participated in the corporate and wholesale banking business only while retail distribution of financial products remained in the hands of domestic players. Bringing Paine Webber into the mix, UBS was now able to tap into its own US distribution channel for financial products created by its wholesale arm. In addition to its clout in the wholesale market, UBS had become a significant force in domestic wealth management. The transformative acquisition of Paine Webber not only drastically increased UBS' footprint in the United States; along with it UBS was put under significantly enhanced scrutiny by US authorities. UBS was no longer a Swiss-based financial institution tipping its toes into the friendly waters of the US market. Owning Paine Webber made it a domestic financial services company in the United States and this warranted a different approach to

inside swiss banking

regulatory oversight and legal scrutiny. Ever since UBS became as much a domestic firm in the US as it was a leading global financial services powerhouse, its exposure to the US legal system grew exponentially, not only with regards to its oversight by regulatory bodies but also with respect to its vulnerability towards US-based litigation.

As we have examined in previous chapters, UBS has experienced the toll that a prolonged dispute in the US legal system can take on their business through their exposure to the great Holocaust debate and the Marcos litigation. While the Marcos class action was shut down in Federal Court, UBS and Credit Suisse saw fit to resolve the Holocaust case with a billion dollar settlement. However, the issues facing UBS in the US tax case were exponentially more difficult and severe than what happened in the Holocaust case. A number of factors were at play that aggravated the situation for UBS. Undoubtedly one of them was the fact that UBS became a significant domestic market force in the early 2000s. With UBS now playing a much more visible role in the domestic wealth management market the US could no longer ignore the offshore business that the firm was engaged in with US persons. For decades the public as well as US authorities had known that US tax payers used offshore banks from the Bahamas to Switzerland to avoid paying taxes in their homeland. The notion that Swiss banks and bankers had been used by tax

135

evaders has long been the stuff that writers of spy novels, movies and investigative journalists feed on. Clandestine Swiss bankers turn up in almost every Ludlum novel or James Bond movie and every so often celebrities will find themselves entangled in a report in Hello Magazine or a publication of equivalent colour on purported problems they may have with tax authorities. One of the most prominent real cases in recent history was the one of Marc Rich, a canny and extremely successful commodities trader who is widely credited with creating the spot market for crude oil. He and a partner established Glencore AG, a company located in Switzerland where Rich elected to make his new home. Living in a secluded mansion on Lake Lucerne, he found himself wanted in the U.S. for illegally trading with Iran and for tax evasion. For years, his name figured prominently on the FBI's fugitive list. The Swiss did not extradite Rich as the crimes he was accused of did not constitute criminal offences in Switzerland. Ever since his indictment in 1983 Rich made sure not to set foot on U.S. soil. In a surprising turn of events of much controversy Marc Rich finally got off the fugitive list when President Bill Clinton granted him a presidential pardon on the last day in office on January 20, 2001. While President Clinton later justified the pardon with legal opinions rendered by prominent law professors at Harvard and Georgetown University, speculations went rampant that the pardon was more related to Rich's valuable connections with the Israeli

inside swiss banking

intelligence community. For years, Rich employed the services of Scooter Libby, a prominent Republican lawyer, as U.S. legal counsel. Libby was part of the inner circle of the incoming Bush Administration which may have given Clinton's pardon some added bi-partisan legitimacy. Even though unrelated to Marc Rich, it is interesting to note that Libby served as presidential advisor to Bush and as Chief of Staff to Cheney from 2001 to 2005 when he was indicted for perjury and obstruction of justice committed in the case of CIA operative Valerie Plame. His 30 month prison term got commuted by President Bush. Having Scooter with a vault of "eyes-only" knowledge in his head spending time in jail was just not an option. As the case of March Rich shows, it is fair to assume that the IRS and other government agencies have known for a long time about the possibility that a bank like UBS might be involved with clients that are not declaring their income from offshore accounts on their IRS returns. With this in mind the question must be asked as to what changed in the global banking equilibrium that caused the IRS and the US DOJ to focus in on UBS in a judicial dragnet that is unparalleled in its aggressiveness and persistence. And why are US authorities singling out UBS vs. other Swiss banks like Credit Suisse, Pictet or Julius Baer? Even though answering these questions will bring us deeply into the realm of speculation it is worth exploring the potential key elements of a constellation that turned so quickly and drastically against one of the leading global financial institutions. We have already touched on the impact of UBS's acquisition of Paine Webber. Not only did this transaction catapult UBS firmly into the domestic wealth management industry; it also needs to be seen in the context of previous corporate transactions made by UBS or one of its predecessor firms, Swiss Bank Corporation (SBC). SBC had its eyes set on the US more decisively than most other Swiss banks. Paine Webber was preceded by noticeable US transactions throughout the 1980s and 1990s. Within a decade SBC gained control over O'Connor Associates in Chicago, a pioneer in developing derivatives, Brinson Partners, a pioneer of a global asset allocation based approach to managing investment portfolios, as well as Dillon Read, one of the leading investment banking boutiques in the North East. The integration of these four businesses into UBS left no doubt with the market or the government that UBS was placing a major bet on being a successful 'bulge bracket' firm in the United States. It also made blatantly clear that UBS was going to take full advantage of the US market opportunities in order to gain further market share globally. This becomes important under the doctrine of 'availing oneself of the US legal system' which gives the US judicial system an anchor for actions against international organizations outside their home jurisdiction. Under this legal doctrine a foreign entity that deliberately avails itself of the US marketplace can be held accountable under the rules of the US legal system if there is no other way to construe US jurisdiction over a foreign entity. Alternatively it can be used to establish a US forum in which to coerce a foreign entity to produce documents or other forms of evidence in the United States even if the evidence resides outside of US jurisdiction. This is to a large degree what the legal issue facing UBS in the Florida Courts was about.

The occurrence of tax evasion via offshore banks has long been a thorn in the side of G8 tax authorities, compounded by the difficulties to access bank information in a complex maze of international treaties. However, the case of an employee at LGT in Liechtenstein providing the German intelligence service with confidential client data caused a change in attitudes. The theft of confidential data by a disgruntled IT technician in Liechtenstein, albeit illegal in the tiny Principality nestled between Rhine River and the Austrian Alps, gave tax investigators all across the G8 an opportunity to harvest data they would, in the normal course of international legal assistance, have had little hope to gain access to. Hundreds of names were suddenly associated with tax offences and a flurry of investigations started in which foreign tax authorities exploited illegally obtained information to go after tax cheats of all walks of life. This data became a cornerstone for the investigation that the U.S. Senate was about to open under the leadership of Senator Carl Levin, a leading Michigan Democrat. The tide had turned and with it the willingness of many justice systems in the G8 to defend due process. The Liechtenstein evidence had after all been gathered in an unlawful act, instigated by a foreign government by way of payment of a hefty bribe. Under normal legal process this would at least raise the question of whether this information was admissible in a criminal investigation. Evidence gathered by the police by raiding a crack house without a valid warrant is thrown out in court even if the ends of getting a drug lord behind bars would seemingly justify the means. The rule of law demands that those who prosecute offences need to stay within the limits of the law at all times. In the now famous LGT case this basic guiding principle of due process appears to have been thrown out the window. What is even more interesting to note is that nobody other than some brave defence lawyers even seems to care. The German government for one has stated officially that the information gathered illegally from LGT will be admissible in German tax investigations. Regardless of the legalities involved here, the LGT case has opened the door in the U.S. for the Senate to establish hearings on tax havens and the extent of tax evasion committed by US persons. For the first time hard evidence had become available on US tax payers holding undeclared assets offshore.

inside swiss banking

As for UBS, an unfortunate chain of events aggravated their situation. While the Senate was busy putting together enough material to strike a committee on tax havens, one of UBS's offshore clients became subject to a well prepared IRS investigation in the process of which his California home was searched and an abundance of documents pertaining to accounts with UBS in Switzerland were seized. As it turned out Igor Olenicoff, a billionaire real estate developer had a knack for keeping meticulous records, even on the UBS accounts that never found their way onto his tax return. Mr. Olenicoff pleaded guilty to a series of tax offences, paid back taxes of $52 million and agreed to repatriate all of his offshore assets to the US, but not without implicating his private banking advisor as a co-conspirator. The advisor, an American citizen named Bradley Birkenfeld had worked for various banks offshore for a couple of decades. When he took on a senior private banking role with UBS in Geneva, he convinced Mr. Olenicoff to move part of his assets over to his new employer. Bradley advised his client on various structuring options regarding his assets, including the use of offshore companies and trusts. Confronted with the prospects of being incarcerated for tax conspiracy, Bradley decided to plead guilty and enter a plea bargain with the IRS, just as his client did. As part of this plea, Mr. Birkenfeld offered to cooperate with the tax investigation and to provide the US authorities with documents and testimony that would

141

support allegations that UBS has made it its business to actively assist US clients in their efforts of evading tax. Bradley Birkenfeld had a few things in common with Igor Olenicoff. Besides the love of a luxurious lifestyle he shared Olenicoff's knack for keeping records. He willingly handed them over to the US authorities and they found their way into the document roster supporting the US Senate hearings on tax havens in 2008. Thanks to Birkenfeld's keen interest in collecting confidential documents, US authorities now had sufficient evidence to support subpoenas for a host of management documents and personal testimony from a number of senior UBS executives in front of the Senate panel. This ultimately gave the Senate Committee access to detailed information on the size of the offshore business that UBS was engaged in with clients across the Americas (US, Canada and Latin America). They also had access to internal policies and procedures regarding travels of UBS relationship managers when meeting with clients in their home jurisdiction. And last but not least there was Birkenfeld's testimony, incriminating UBS as a firm, as well as the senior executives in charge of offshore private banking, with directing him and other relationship managers to assist clients in their efforts to avoid detection. The unprecedented chain of events from the theft of data in Liechtenstein to the catch of Olenicoff and Birkenfeld in an IRS dragnet emboldened the political and the judicial wing of the US legal system to lay out a conspiracy case

inside swiss banking

against UBS. The world leader in global wealth management had been caught in the act of aggressively pursuing offshore business opportunities with US residents. What is more, documents put on file with the US Senate support a view that in its pursuit of US clients, UBS may have been acting outside of the confines of US law. As an organization that very publicly availed itself of the US market, UBS was under increased scrutiny. The detection of dubious business practices when dealing with US offshore clients was naturally something that required further attention. Cynical analysts would add to this that the market meltdown of 2008 and 2009 created favourable timing to go after UBS aggressively. After all, UBS was the one bank outside of the US that was hit the hardest by the financial sector crisis in the aftermath of sub-prime mortgages. UBS had lost the staggering sum of over \$40bn, more than any other European bank and more than most banks in the US. It paid a hefty price for its obsession with becoming a top three player in the US fixed income market and in early 2009 was teetering on the brink of extinction before receiving a \$6 billion shot in the arm by the Swiss Government. This created weakness, made the bank vulnerable and potentially more open to cooperate with US judicial procedures.

In summary, UBS was indeed in a special situation as far as its relationship with the US was concerned. It was the most aggressive of all Swiss banks in the US market and had the misfortune of employing Mr. Birkenfeld, who turned out to be an unexpected source of confidential information on its offshore business with Americans. Through Birkenfeld's testimony, UBS found itself caught in the act of violating US banking and securities regulations and turning a blind eye to private bankers that conspired with their clients in committing tax offences. And lastly, UBS was severely troubled in its financial condition through the misadventures in the US fixed income market which made it easy prey for the American judiciary.

The US judicial system is better equipped to coerce cooperation with court proceedings than most other legal frameworks around the globe. US judges have a host of measures at their disposal with which to enforce compliance. They have a degree of latitude and discretion in applying these measures that is unique within most democracies, globally. While defending their position in the Marcos class action, Swiss Bank Corporation and Credit Suisse had made their experience with sometimes arbitrary decisions made by Mr. Justice Manuel Real, the flamboyant judge of the 9th Federal Circuit. But what unfolded in Los Angeles and Hawaii in the 1990s was a walk in the park compared to the nightmare of the proceedings opened by the US Justice Department and a Miami court in 2008 and

inside swiss banking

2009. The severity with which the US Courts would proceed against UBS seems to indicate that they were emboldened by the unique situation that the Swiss bank found itself in: financially weakened and fully exposed by the evidence that had been handed over to the US Senate. Swiss banks had had their issues with US judicial or regulatory authorities in the past but those proceedings were mostly conducted and resolved in a civilized manner. Now things seemed to get personal. It all started in the early summer of 2008 when Martin Liechti, Head at UBS Private Banking for The Americas was traveling through Miami International Airport on his way back to Switzerland from a trip to South America. His stop in Miami was not scheduled even though he was a frequent visitor to Southern Florida. UBS had a large office in Miami dealing mainly with South American clients. Due to its central location Miami was also one of the preferred locations to hold management conferences for The Americas business region. This time, however, Martin Liechti had no reason to land in Miami other than the fact that he needed to reschedule his flight back to Switzerland from a business trip further south. Routing through Miami was the only option. This turned out to be an eventful change of plans. Immediately after setting foot on US soil, Liechti was apprehended by US Marshals. The Miami court investigating the allegations that UBS conspired with its clients in evading US tax had ordered Liechti to be detained as a material witness. This

145

step was truly unprecedented. Mr. Liechti was not charged with any wrong doing but this could change rapidly now that the authorities had him detained on US territory. For several weeks his ability to move was restricted to the confines of the Miami luxury hotel he was made to stay at. One step too far and his ankle bracelet would get him arrested for violation of the detention order. During the course of his involuntary vacation in Miami Martin Liechti appeared in front of the US Senate hearing and received the type of hostile grilling he had to expect after the Justice Department had taken away his freedom of movement. His testimony was likely not as fruitful as the Senate Committee or the Justice Department had hoped. He was briefed and coached well by U.S. counsel and made use of the Fifth Amendment in the U.S. Constitution rather than liberally providing insights into the operation of UBS in Switzerland. 'Taking the Fifth' was the only way for him to avoid prosecution in Swiss courts for violating bank secrecy laws. The detention of Mr. Liechti and leaving him in the legal limbo that comes with being qualified a material witness was effective nevertheless. UBS now knew how seriously the tax case was going to play out. The U.S. would go and push UBS into submission by taking any and all measures available to its judiciary. With the U.S. adopting a 'no holds barred' attitude, this case was not going to be civilized. Exposure of the offshore business to the U.S. had to be minimized to avoid giving the U.S. more unintended

inside swiss banking

leverage and so UBS decided to stop all unnecessary travel. American offshore clients would no longer be visited and no business development was going to take place on U.S. soil. In fact, UBS decided to discontinue its offshore business with U.S. based clients altogether, giving up about $20 billion in assets and $200 million in revenues. In a legal system that turned hostile to the degree it had over the course of 2008, the legal risks involved in conducting business as usual were no longer worth taking.

While Martin Liechti was happy to be reunited with his family after several weeks of detention in Florida, UBS decided that he could no longer continue to serve in his role as Head of Americas. The U.S. detention turned him into damaged goods; the brief, unscheduled stop-over in Miami had ended his career as executive at the world's largest wealth management firm. The same fate reached Martin's boss in November of 2008. Raoul Weil had an extremely successful career at Swiss Bank Corporation and subsequently at UBS. He joined SBC in 1984 right out of University and moved through the ranks in various departments before he took over the Private Banking division at SBC New York in the mid 1990s. After successfully turning around the faltering division, he was awarded a position to lead SBC's fast-growing business in Asia in 1997, a position he held on to after the UBS merger. A promotion to Head of Private Banking International followed. Raoul became chief executive over all offshore business as well as the domestic businesses outside of Switzerland. He ultimately ended up as Chief Executive Officer of the bank's overall Wealth Management and Business Banking unit when Marcel Rohner became CEO of the bank to replace Peter Wuffli who had to take the fall for the early losses in the US credit market crisis in 2007. Weil's illustrious career ended abruptly on November 6, 2008 when the U.S. DOJ indicted him of conspiracy to assist 20,000 Americans in the evasion of U.S. tax. Again, the damaging and compromising documentation that had been surrendered to the Senator Levin's Committee on Tax Havens provided the U.S. authorities with enough ammunition to put together a case against the man that was in charge of global wealth management, UBS's most profitable business. Weil was the man under whose watch all the transgressions occurred. He was the ultimately responsible executive for Birkenfeld's escapades of hiding diamonds in a tube of toothpaste to avoid a paper trail that would link Igor Olenicoff to accounts at UBS in Switzerland. He was also the man that the Justice Department chose to pin the damaging policy regarding trips by UBS bankers outside of Switzerland on. This policy focused more on instructing bankers how not to get caught than it did on ensuring that all activities of the bank outside of Switzerland would comply with local rules. It reads more like a spy novel than a risk and compliance policy and it

inside swiss banking

created the need for UBS to do a lot of explaining once it had seen the daylight of the public Senate proceedings and the media attention that comes with it. The Miami court in charge of the tax case against UBS decided that the buck was going to stop with Raoul and raised the stakes in the legal attack against UBS at the same time. While Martin Liechti was simply detained as a material witness and let go after a few weeks of intimidation, the modus operandi changed with regards to Raoul Weil. He was personally indicted as a co-conspirator in countless current and future tax evasion cases and coerced to appear in front of the Miami court, not as a witness, but as an accused. Needless to say, Raoul did not take any chances in complying with the summons to appear in Miami but on the advice of counsel decided to vigorously defend against the indictment from the comfort of his home. The Swiss prosecutors would not force him to appear in the United States and a voluntary appearance in Florida would expose him to the risk of detention as he would likely be considered a flight risk. As long as Weil would stay in Switzerland, the execution of the indictment against him would have to occur within the framework of international law and specific treaties that exist between Switzerland and the U.S. Weil had no reason to give up the protection of his rights under Swiss and international law by voluntarily subjecting himself to an unpredictable and possibly arbitrary legal process in Florida, presided over by a judge with the widest of discretion to make his life miserable. This may have irritated the judge expecting Mr. Weil to step in front of the bench in Miami. His failure to comply with the summons to appear on the specified date was not taken as a sign that Mr. Weil was simply protecting his civil liberties. It was seen as an effort by Mr. Weil to escape U.S. jurisdiction. To raise the bar further in a battle that had already gotten as nasty as it could, Raoul Weil was declared a fugitive on January 13, 2009. He was now on the list of law enforcement agencies across the United States and in every country that the US has an extradition agreement with. The indictment in the U.S. had not only ended his career but also his mobility. As a fugitive he could not risk setting foot outside of his home jurisdiction without fear of extradition; a tough fate for a globetrotting individual that had racked up hundreds of thousands of frequent flyer miles over the past couple of decades.

While US prosecutors were going after Liechti and Weil on a personal level, the DOJ threatened to formally bring criminal charges against UBS in case the bank decided not to hand over documents pertaining to accounts held for US taxpayers. Based on an earlier petition by the DOJ, a federal judge in Miami had issued an order on July 1, 2008 authorizing the IRS to request that UBS provide information about U.S. clients who may have been using bank accounts in Switzerland to evade federal income

inside swiss banking

taxes. In its subsequent "John Doe" summons to UBS, the IRS failed to establish on what grounds the assumption was made that the 52,000 accounts that were subject to the order were all suspicious of tax evasion or tax fraud. Such unsubstantiated requests for information violate the provisions of the mutual legal assistance laws in Switzerland. UBS would break Swiss law if it chose to comply with the summons in its present form. UBS was faced with the typical dilemma of any banking institution that is active in cross-border business: compliance with Swiss law would create contempt of court in the U.S. and compliance with the "John Doe" summons in the U.S. would make UBS and its executives open to prosecution in Switzerland for violation of bank secrecy laws. The DOJ and the IRS must have been aware that bringing the "John Doe" summons against UBS amounted to a game of ultimate jeopardy. But the stakes were high from the outset of the case. Neither the DOJ nor the IRS had any inclination of going along with the tedious and time consuming process laid out under the bilateral agreements between the U.S. and Switzerland regarding the exchange of information in tax matters. Bradley Birkenfeld and the testimony of a myriad of UBS executives at the Senate hearings had given them too much advanced information. Combined with the bank's financial and reputational weakness, nobody would resist the temptation to test the bank's stamina and its commitment to participation in the

U.S. marketplace. Threatening UBS to bring criminal charges against it as a conspirator to defraud the U.S. would no doubt get the attention of the bank's Board and Chief Executive. If granted, the criminal charges would turn UBS into a criminal organization with the stroke of a federal judge's pen. Whether or not UBS was actually culpable or convictable was a secondary concern. The fact of the matter was that UBS would face severe damage by loosing current clients and being avoided for future business. Nobody in the U.S. or elsewhere would want to business with a criminally branded organization, especially not a bank where good reputation, trust and reliability played such a critical role. UBS was faced with a $40 billion loss and threatening liquidity shortage in the market. In this context a criminal conspiracy charge against the bank had the potential to put UBS out of business very quickly. The market recognized the severity of the threat and caused UBS to drop 14 percent in value in a single session on the Zurich and New York exchanges. UBS was forced into a triple balancing act as its next steps had to consider consequences under Swiss and U.S. law as well as implications any decisions would have on the very viability of the bank. Peter Kurer, UBS Chairman and Marcel Rohner, the bank's Chief Executive Officer knew that no matter how hard they tried, the bank would not get out of this situation unharmed. On top of the trouble the bank was in, both Kurer and Rohner would have felt threatened

inside swiss banking

on a personal level as well. Who was to say that the DOJ would content itself with having Raoul Weil immobilized by indicting him with conspiracy charges in the United States and subsequently declaring him a fugitive? Without significant movement on the part of UBS to resolve the impasse, Rohner and Kurer might be next on the list of key individuals the DOJ was going to go after. Losing Weil within the senior ranks of the bank was one thing but the risk of an indictment of its CEO and potentially its Chairman would add a completely new dimension that needed to be avoided at all cost.

The threat to the bank's very existence was real, not only to the bank's executive team and its shareholders, but also in the eyes of the Swiss financial market regulator, FINMA. If criminal charges were successfully brought against UBS this would not only threaten the viability of the nation's largest bank. There was a potential for future trouble at Credit Suisse and any other Swiss bank with an active book of business in the United States. The prospect of having UBS criminally charged in the U.S. was a matter of national interest as it threatened the future of Switzerland as an international financial centre and as the leading hub for cross-border private banking. Acting through FINMA the Swiss government had to do something to avert the Tsunami that was well on its way from Washington to Bern. FINMA and UBS had worked collaboratively in a regulatory investigation into the bank's conduct of business under the Qualified Intermediary Agreement. Based on this investigation and the bank's own efforts, it did appear as though some 300 of the 52,000 accounts affected by the "John Doe" summons were highly likely linked to fraudulent activity of the account holders which made these accounts accessible to the IRS in a legal assistance procedure, if such procedures were ever going to be initiated. Using the existing distinction in Swiss criminal law between tax fraud and tax evasion, FINMA decided to short circuit the legal assistance process and on February 18, 2009 ordered UBS to hand over documents on the 300 accounts that had been identified as potentially exposed to fraud allegations. The violation of the account holders' rights of due process and habeas corpus was accepted as collateral damage in an effort to secure the stability of the Swiss financial system and to protect the interests of creditors and shareholders of UBS. The FINMA order paved the way for UBS entering into a deferred prosecution agreement with the DOJ the same day. Therein UBS agreed to expeditiously exit the business of providing offshore banking services to US clients and to pay $780 million in fines, penalties, interest and restitution. With this agreement the threat of a criminal charge was successfully eliminated. The deferred prosecution agreement did not include the "John Doe" summons in its non-criminal component and it excluded the case against former UBS executive Raoul Weil.

inside swiss banking

These two cases continued and created significant disturbance between the two governments. UBS had been coming clean on a number of levels in its unlawful activities in the United States, spanning from doing business in the U.S. without proper licensing by the SEC to actively advising clients on tax avoidance strategies. The bank paid a substantial fine and offered its cooperation with the ongoing investigation; the expectation after all this was that the bank should no longer be considered an organization that dodges U.S. laws and securities regulations but should be given the respect of an organization that operates in good faith. The DOJ and the Swiss government engaged in a very active effort to find common ground to settle the outstanding issues over several months. However, doubt continued to linger as to whether the Federal Judge presiding over the case in Florida would go along with an increasing desire to deal with the issues at hand on a level that was more inspired by diplomacy among the world's two oldest democracies than by a unilateral demonstration of American judicial power.

The "John Doe" summons raises significant concerns among those who are interested in maintaining an international legal framework in which jurisdictional borders are respected. The judicial procedure in Florida is based on the simple assumption that any U.S. resident that banks with UBS in Switzerland is automatically suspected of committing a tax offence. The fact that someone opened a bank account with a leading global financial institution in Switzerland serves as probable cause to open a blanket tax process covering all 52,000 account holders at UBS in Switzerland that are considered to be U.S. persons. The "John Doe" summons does not substantiate what the IRS or the DOJ consider being probable cause; UBS was simply ordered to surrender any and all account information it had on file regarding the alleged 52,000 accounts held at UBS for U.S. persons. It was clear from the outset that this type of legal procedure had no chance of being granted the privilege of international legal assistance through Swiss authorities. So the DOJ and the IRS chose a route that forced UBS to comply with the summons directly in the U.S., regardless of the implications such compliance would have under Swiss law. The US courts, hungry for the information that will allow them to establish probable cause in hundreds of tax evasion cases, evidently did not care about the concerns that some experts have regarding the civilized exchange of due legal process across borders. The "John Doe" summons was nothing but a show of power of the mighty United States and its determination to use its legal system in an imperialistic fashion in a case important enough for the ends to justify the means. The notion that a U.S. person with a bank account in Switzerland should be presumed guilty of tax evasion until they can prove their innocence flies in the face of one of the most basic

inside swiss banking

principles in law. It potentially subjects law abiding citizens to prosecution by the IRS for tax crimes or other tax related offences that have never been committed. Among the many different groups of foreigners that have some of their money under the custody of Swiss banks, North American clients have been known for decades as the one group with the highest rate of tax compliance. While the banks have no obligation to verify whether clients include their Swiss-based accounts in their home country tax returns, American and Canadian clients have long been recognized as those who do so more often than any other clients. The banks would have had plenty indication to that effect from the fact that North American clients have asked for information relevant to their tax returns more frequently than clients residing in France or Germany. Banks like UBS had to produce year-end statements on income and capital gains for these clients long before such reports became standard practice and they did so in a manual process. They have known for decades that the basic assumption leading to the "John Doe" summons is inaccurate. On the other hand it is probably fair to say that the private bankers advising U.S. clients at UBS in Zurich would have some degree of knowledge on which clients likely are tax offenders. Even though the use of complex offshore legal structures per se is no give-away for unlawful activity, it usually raises the question as to why a client would choose to hold their assets in multiple levels of holding companies and trusts. The answer may well be unrelated to tax but often these structures will have been chosen to keep certain assets out of reach of tax authorities in an aggressive tax planning effort engineered by U.S. and international accountants and lawyers. The "John Doe" summons does not bother giving consideration to these kinds of distinctions. It specifically does not limit the information request to cases where the bank has knowledge or reason to believe that a specific client is most likely engaged in banking activities offshore that violate their reporting requirements in the U.S. Were UBS to comply with the summons and surrender all US client data to the IRS, such disclosure of data would not only violate Swiss law, it would most likely expose thousands of American clients to groundless and unnecessary prosecution by the IRS. Thousands of perfectly tax compliant U.S. persons would have to establish innocence against the presumed guilt by association derived from the fact that they operate one of 52,000 offshore accounts with UBS. And in doing so they will have to carry thousands of dollars in unnecessary legal costs; a subtlety that is of no concern to the DOJ or the IRS. Law abiding individuals being caught in the IRS dragnet is just collateral damage that, while deplorable in the individual situation, is deemed unavoidable in the big scheme of the campaign against offshore banking.

inside swiss banking

The aggressive course of action against UBS has further created an unprecedented level of voluntary disclosures by clients that would rather make a deal with the IRS before the bank's potential surrendering of data. These clients' settlements with the IRS include an agreement to pay back taxes and penalties in exchange for a full discharge by the IRS. There is no valid reason for accounts that have been subject to a voluntary disclosure settlement to be included in the summons. The IRS has nothing further to investigate or prosecute in these cases.

As we have explored in previous chapters, high net worth individuals may find placing assets with banks in Switzerland to be a good idea for reasons unrelated to taxation or the avoidance thereof. The privacy laws contained in the Swiss Bank Act can serve to protect assets legitimately for a rainy day. Jurisdictions with strong secrecy laws such as Switzerland or Singapore have long been attractive locations to keep certain assets in creditor proof structures. This is especially true for assets that are exposed to high risks related to frivolous litigation practices condoned by courts. The United States are a prime example of this class of jurisdiction. U.S. based clients may find it simply good estate planning to protect certain assets in an offshore location and they don't have to break any U.S. laws to do so. Other U.S. persons may have spent several years of their professional lives in Europe working as

159

expatriate executives for international corporations. They may have had a bank account with a Swiss bank to facilitate the financial aspects of their life in Europe or other parts of the world outside of the U.S. And they may have decided to keep these accounts in place even after moving back to the United States. During their expatriate stay in Europe they may have grown accustomed to investing assets in equity markets outside of the U.S. and in structured products offered by Swiss or other European banks that had little correlation to the United States. American banks and investment firms would not be able to support these investments with the same level of service quality as a Swiss bank can. U.S. financial institutions are by nature focused on the United States markets and their expertise in global markets, specifically Europe, pales in comparison to the leading Swiss and European-based institutions. As long as the income and capital gains realized from such accounts find its way into the appropriate U.S. tax return no unlawful acts have been committed. Why would these types of accounts have to be exposed to the judicial process emanating from the "John Doe" procedure? It makes no sense to declare all the law abiding U.S. clients at UBS guilty by association with those who have broken the law.

The "John Doe" summons is legally questionable because it is based on inaccurate assumptions. It does not hold on closer inspection under international

inside swiss banking

law. It violates privacy rights of law abiding citizens and overshoots the purpose of the IRS investigation which is to bring tax cheats to justice. These concerns of an outside legal perspective did not hinder the U.S. from demonstrating to the Swiss and the world how far they will go in enforcing their rule of law regardless of international borders and generally accepted rules of international law. If the case evolving from the "John Doe" summons was ever going to be resolved by way of an out-of-court settlement the U.S wanted to have a pound of Swiss flesh. UBS made it known early on in the process that a settlement was their preferred course of action. Their dilemma, however was that they would have to make sure that whatever they agree to accept as a settlement of the "John Doe" summons will be compatible with Swiss law. The Swiss Government chose a dual course of action. On the one hand it supported UBS in its defence against the Miami court orders with various interventions and amicus curiae briefs outlining the conflict of law between two sovereign states that was coming to the fore in this case. On the other hand, just as settlement talks heated up during the summer of 2009, the Swiss Federal Council released a statement that it would prohibit the release of any client data to the IRS under any such settlement if and when such transfer of data were to violate Swiss law. The Swiss Government received quite a bit of criticism from the media and politicians as it was unclear why it would make such a big story out of stating the obvious, namely that Switzerland was going to uphold its own laws. Was the Federal Government seriously concerned that UBS was embarked on doing a deal with the Department of Justice that would lead to a violation of Swiss secrecy laws? Or was the Federal Council just making it clear to the U.S. Government that it will take any measures necessary to uphold Swiss sovereignty in case the United States were pushing too hard? Whatever the reasoning of the Federal Council, the elevation of the issue to the level of two sovereign nations worked. For weeks, government officials from both countries formed a number of joint task forces to find a solution outside of the courts to the mess that UBS had manoeuvred itself into. At the same time, Swiss and U.S. officials worked on an updated version of the U.S.-Swiss Tax Treaty as part of the Swiss effort to respond to the increasing pressure from the OECD. The new tax treaty, signed in October of 2009 now contains provisions that allow legal assistance not only in tax fraud but also in tax evasion cases, provided the IRS lays out probable cause.

Just before UBS was publishing its half-year results for 2009 the Swiss and U.S. Governments jointly declared on July 31st that the two administrations had worked out a protocol by which to settle the dispute about the "John Doe" Summons. To underline the importance of the agreement, Secretary of State Clinton and her Swiss

inside swiss banking

counterpart Calmy-Rey made the announcement in person. An unprecedented balancing act of sovereign interests between the United States and Switzerland, the agreement provides a framework that enables UBS to release certain client documents under established international legal assistance protocols. It is to be expected that affected U.S. clients of UBS will challenge any disclosures made by UBS under this framework until all opportunities for appeal are exhausted. The flow of client data to the IRS will not be immediate and in certain cases will take years to materialize. However, for UBS the Damocles sword of the "John Doe" summons disappeared. For all the other Swiss banks doing business with U.S. clients offshore, a protocol for access to client information by U.S. authorities has now been established.

On August 19th, 2009 the Swiss Federal Council announced the details of the agreement reached with the United States regarding cooperation in the UBS tax case. In summary, the agreement states that in exchange for a withdrawal of the "John Doe" summons in the Federal Court in Miami, Switzerland will provide the IRS with access to some 4500 client files. This represents around 8 percent of the 52,000 accounts that had been made the subject of the summons. Access to these files will be granted based on a new request for administrative assistance that the U.S. will submit to the Swiss government under the existing tax treaty between the two countries. Affected clients will be able to appeal any decisions made in their regard and such appeals will go directly to the highest administrative court in Switzerland for final decision. To expedite execution of the administrative assistance process Switzerland will hire additional staff and contract tax and accounting specialists with the objective to have all 4500 cases closed within a year, not considering any appeals by affected clients. The case filed in the U.S. against UBS will be dropped and UBS will not pay any additional fines. This settlement is astonishing in that it gives all parties involved areas of victory: the U.S. will get access to a significant number of files and keep the pressure high on American taxpayers to come clean in a voluntary disclosure program especially designed for those with bank accounts in Switzerland. Switzerland successfully maintains sovereignty over the issue of providing banking information across its border. The exchange of information will be governed by Swiss law and the Swiss-U.S. tax treaty. UBS gets rid of the most damaging claim it has ever faced and can move on to fixing its business. In addition to all this, the agreement sets the stage for any further information requests that the DOJ and the IRS will want to place with their Swiss counterparties in the future. After all, UBS is not the only bank dealing with American clients. Banks like Credit Suisse, Julius Baer, Pictet and all the others will take some comfort from the bilateral settlement as it sets out the

inside swiss banking

ground rules for what may well come their way in the near future.

Ever since Senator Levin had started his investigation, the DOJ and the IRS have taken an aggressive stance against UBS. Emboldened by the evidence in front of the U.S. Senate, they chose to go after the bank in the U.S. rather than going down the long and tedious path of legal assistance from Switzerland. The question has to be asked then, why the U.S. negotiation team finally accepted the notion that the flow of client information to the IRS will have to occur under Swiss law and according to the principles set out in the bilateral tax treaty. Why did the U.S. finally give up jurisdiction over UBS in this case? The answer will have to be somewhat speculative as details of the negotiations are not public. Speculation or hard fact, it is worth exploring what political, legal and economic consideration may have driven the parties to reaching a deal. In the initial stages of the U.S. tax scandal UBS tried to appease the American side by signalling cooperation. The bank volunteered testimony at the Senate hearings, delivered binders full of documentation and assured the courts of its willingness to comply with what is asked of the bank provided they could do so without violating Swiss law. In February of 2009, the Swiss financial markets regulator even came to the rescue when it ordered UBS under Swiss emergency laws to surrender 300 or so client files without

165

allowing the affected clients to appeal before the data transfer. The concerted appeasement effort by the bank and the Swiss regulator was not answered with acts of gratitude in the U.S. To the contrary, it was interpreted as a sign of weakness in the face of pressure and led to the issuance of the "John Doe" summons. Appeasement did not work; if anything it emboldened the IRS to launch the biggest fishing expedition in the history of the agency and the District Judge in Miami to back the expedition up with the fire power of the US judicial system. Why not? After all, UBS had admitted to wrongdoing in the deferred prosecution agreements signed the same day that FINMA took control over the 300 tax fraud files. It had also paid the stiff fine of $780 million further cementing its admission of guilt. The bullying tactics including the detention of Martin Liechti and the indictment of Raoul Weil had provided the desired outcomes and the U.S. had no reason to stop now. This was as good a time as ever to go for the kill. The weakened UBS had successfully been brought to its knees and the Swiss financial market regulator was ready to play along with the tactics employed by the American government.

What the DOJ and the federal judge sitting in Miami did not realize was that at some point even the conservative, neutral and cooperative Swiss would decide that enough was enough. UBS had gone through wholesale

inside swiss banking

change in its senior leadership. The guilty conscience of its former Chairman and executive team no longer served as the driver of decision making. UBS brought in a tough, experienced no-nonsense executive as its new CEO after Marcel Rohner resigned from the position in early 2009. Oswald Gruebel had turned around a messy Credit Suisse several years earlier and established a reputation as someone who was tough enough to do what was necessary. A straight-talking German grown up in the GDR, his direct style has made him a much feared but equally respected business leader. He could and would start with a clean slate and take a much tougher stance with regards to the issues facing UBS in the United States. In addition, UBS brought in Kaspar Villiger as its new Chairman in April of 2009. Mr. Villiger was a former member of the Swiss Federal Council from 1989 to 2003, during which time he served as Defence and Finance Minister. In his role as Federal Councillor he was no stranger to cleaning up after scandals. In 1989, he succeeded the first woman to ever get elected to the Federal Council. Elisabeth Kopp was Justice Minister since her election in 1984 and in 1989 a confidential memo linking her husband to (unsubstantiated) allegations of money laundering forced her to resign. Kaspar Villiger was the right choice for a tough job at UBS; he had the experience and connections of a long-standing member of Federal government. Kaspar Villiger had retired from politics in 2003 and served on the Board of Nestle and Swiss Re when he got the phone call from UBS. His global connections are best exemplified by his senior leadership role in the illustrious circle of the "Global Leadership Foundation", an organization dedicated to promote good governance across the globe and advise heads of state on related matters. Mr. Villiger's peers at the "GLF" include, among others, William F. De Klerk of South Africa, Jose Maria Aznar of Spain, Lord Patten of the UK and Hong Kong, Fidel Ramos of the Philippines, Joe Clark of Canada and last but not least Chester Crocker of the US, a name we have come across earlier in the discussion of the Marcos files. Kaspar Villiger is not your typical recycled politician and his appointment to the helm of the troubled bank was not going to be a plum job for a few years. He was brought in with a purpose and he agreed to put the full weight of his political and governance experience behind the Chairmanship at the bank. With Gruebel and Villiger, UBS had put in place the kind of energized new leadership team that was necessary to achieve the turnaround. Both men enjoy indisputable reputations and respect in the Swiss and global communities. There was an unmistakeable wind of change at UBS head office in Zurich, noticeable not only within the bank but also to the public and politicians. The new mood caught on with the government when the Swiss Federal Council declared in the spring of 2009 that it would prohibit UBS from complying with any court orders issued in the United States if such compliance would result in UBS

inside swiss banking

violating Swiss law. The time of appeasement was over. Instead, the Swiss government changed tactics and took an active approach in defending sovereignty over its legal and judicial system in the face of the unrelenting attacks from across the Atlantic.

And this is where speculation starts: What did the Swiss government have up their sleeve that made the U.S. negotiators change tactics and ultimately cave in to the demands that whatever information was going to be disclosed, the process had to follow the framework of Swiss law? My own interpretation is that, as the file was escalated up the chain of bilateral diplomacy, the quality of mutual interests that were thrown in the balance had changed. This was no longer just a dispute about how the U.S. would deal with UBS and how the Swiss government was going to protect the country's largest financial institution. It had become a discussion as to how the dispute might affect future relations between two nations that had a long-standing and friendly history. The Swiss government had good arguments to put the whole political and diplomatic relationship on the table in order to restore the balance. Having already committed to renegotiate international tax treaties with the U.S. as well as other key nations, there was no longer a need to act from a defensive position only. Switzerland is a small country of just over seven million people with a territory half the size of the State of Maine

169

but as we explored earlier in this chapter, the Swiss and the Americans share a specific democratic tradition that creates a special bond. These friendly relations have led to special diplomatic relations as well, as evidenced by Switzerland delivering diplomatic services on behalf of the U.S. in Iran and Cuba. This makes the tiny confederation in the Alps an important partner to the mighty United States of America. Considering this, the Swiss had added weight to put into the balance. First there was UBS and its importance as an employer in the U.S. The bank employs over 34,000 people in the US, more than Morgan Stanley or Goldman Sachs. If no way could be found to end the court proceedings against UBS in the Miami Federal District, the bank may have been forced to close its U.S. operations altogether. This would have been a painful exercise for UBS. It would also have added a significant number of job losses in the U.S. and enabled UBS to stonewall against the fishing expedition by the IRS for years to come, with the full support of the Swiss government. Secondary considerations had no relationship with UBS but were a matter of bilateral diplomatic relationships. As the Obama administration was looking to close Guantanamo the US called in favours from friendly nations to take a few of the inmates so it did not have to bring all of the suspected terrorists into the Homeland. Switzerland was on that list and had offered to help early in 2009. It could easily make its willingness to cooperate conditional on a satisfactory outcome of the UBS case.

inside swiss banking

Losing Switzerland as a destination for "Gitmo" inmates would be a blow to the effectiveness of U.S. diplomacy and could lead other friendly nations to reconsider their position as well. But the most critical role that Bern played for Washington was the one in Tehran. Without Swiss representation, Washington had no diplomatic back-channel access to a rogue nation that, next to the regime of Kim Jong Il, is generally seen as the most serious threat to global stability. The U.S. had broken off diplomatic relations with Iran in April of 1980, shortly after the Islamic Revolution of 1979 and as a reaction to the U.S. hostage crisis in Tehran that led to President Carter's loss in the Presidential Election of 1979 to Ronald Reagan. Switzerland assumed representation of American interest in Iran in 1981. 28 years later, Iran is still a wild card with nuclear ambitions and an unhidden agenda of aggression against Israel. It could not possibly be in America's interest to lose the good services of Swiss diplomats over a tax dispute; certainly not in the new era that the Obama administration brought after Bush in which a fresh approach was going to be taken on relations with Iran. Therefore, the Tehran-Bern-Washington triangle of diplomacy would undoubtedly have been a key bargaining chip for Swiss negotiators in the UBS tax case.

Regardless of whether any of these speculative considerations in fact served as actual background for this

171

settlement, it is a good example as to how seemingly irreconcilable differences can be resolved in a way that gives all parties involved a win. It would not be a surprise to find this U.S./Swiss agreement used in case studies of major Universities as a show case of successful negotiation and dispute resolution.

While UBS and the Swiss government can look back on a relatively satisfactory resolution of the US tax case, the same can not be said for Bradley Birkenfeld and Raoul Weil. Birkenfeld had hoped that his cooperation with the prosecution of UBS would get him whistleblower status and the leniency of the courts that usually goes with it. However, Birkenfeld forgot that whistleblowers usually come forward with information without being in the crosshairs of the authorities and that on this account, he would not qualify. It was Igor Olenicoff that identified Bradley as his banking advisor in an effort to deflect responsibility for the committed tax offences on UBS and the banker that was looking after his affairs. So, Bradley's noble offer to assist US prosecutors with their case against his former employer as not so voluntary after all. Birkenfeld was arrested even after pleading guilty and eventually sentenced to a 40 month prison term for one count of fraud conspiracy. Unlike his client, who pleaded guilty and paid in excess of $52 million in back-taxes and fines without being sent to jail, he had no money to offer to settle his case. The hard-nosed treatment of Birkenfeld by the DOJ and the courts irates organizations such as the National Whistleblower Centre. The NAC and some other advocacy groups intervened in October of 2009 with US Attorney General Eric Holder to review Bradley's case and it remains to be seen whether the U.S. government will come to his support. There is little hope in this regard for Raoul Weil, the former CEO of UBS's wealth management operations. His case is still open as he remains a fugitive as he became collateral damage in the settlement between UBS, the Swiss government and the United States.

CHAPTER SIXTEEN

The European Union Riding on US Coat Tails

The UBS tax case in the United States has created a situation in which the European Union and most importantly Germany have started to sense an opportunity to close in on tax evasion committed by their own citizen via offshore banking in Switzerland and other 'tax havens' such as Luxembourg and Austria. The sense of urgency that prevailed in the Swiss Government's reaction to the threat to the very existence of UBS in February of 2009 caused an increased appetite within the German administration to push hard against the Swiss Confederation. The German Finance Minister and some of his senior colleagues in the Social Democratic Party found words to describe the Swiss that nobody had used for over sixty years. Memories from a not so glorious past in German history resurfaced when German ministers mused publicly that the easiest way to force the Swiss into cooperation might be to send troops South across the Rhine River. The picture of Nazi tanks rolling towards the Swiss border was painted vividly in a

inside swiss banking

special session of the Swiss Parliament that was urgently assembled in response to the hostilities coming from Berlin. Luckily, the discussion got toned down rapidly after German officials realized that in the views of some of their neighbours Berlin was still sitting in the glass house that Hitler and his Nazi cronies had built for the children of the German "Wirtschaftswunder". Cooler heads prevailed soon enough in the bilateral war of words between Bern and Berlin, maybe as a result of other European nations reminding Germany that the attacks on its southerly neighbour had definitely crossed the limits of what was acceptable in a political fight. Gordon Brown, the British Prime Minister, stood out as the leader among the European politicians favouring an effort to end the path of isolating Switzerland and bring the discussion on cross-border tax back to the mainstream of friendly diplomacy. After all, Switzerland was much more valuable as a partner willing to try and find a way to increase cooperation in cross-border tax matters than as a nation pushing back against the attacks on its sovereignty.

Faced with the enormous international pressure of a concerted effort by the U.S., the EU and the OECD the Swiss Federal Council declared on March 13th, 2009 that Switzerland will give up the distinction of tax fraud and tax evasion in dealings with foreign nationals. This decision by the Federal Government allowed Switzerland to keep sovereignty internally as the domestic tax laws remain unchanged while externally the interpretation of Swiss tax laws was being brought in line with international standards. A sybillinic solution to be sure. For one, it restored credibility of Switzerland's foreign relations by giving up a legal technicality that had grown increasingly indefensible. It was also the only way for the Swiss Government to get the support from Parliament to implement the changes to international tax treaty law resulting from the policy shift. Within only a few months Switzerland engaged in discussions with all of its major trading partners about changes to existing tax treaties that would allow for an exchange of information in tax evasion cases. This effort to cooperate more openly with the EU got Switzerland off the black and grey lists that the OECD had published in preparation of the G8 tax summit in London in the spring of 2009. The pressure that the United States, Germany, the EU and the OECD put on Switzerland has clearly yielded a positive result for them. The Swiss came to the conclusion that upholding the distinction of criminal tax fraud and non-criminal tax evasion was not a defendable position in the long run; at least not with respect to dealings with those who were subject to taxation in a foreign country. While Switzerland will keep drawing the line of criminal and non-criminal tax offences internally, it had to signal to the global community that the country and its banks were not designed to harbour international tax offenders. By the

inside swiss banking

same token, the European Union and Germany in particular need to realize that international cooperation in tax matters will have to be governed by a protocol that is acceptable to all parties involved. Switzerland will stick to its underlying philosophy that tax compliance is an individual duty of the tax payer and that banks will not be used to police taxpayers on behalf of the Revenue Department. Most EU nations have a different approach in which bank information that is relevant for tax purposes is fed to the tax authorities by automated data link. This leads to fully transparent banking relationships and minimizes the privacy that bank clients can expect from their bankers. This type of information exchange is as incompatible with the Swiss tax system as introducing an obligation for employers to deduct employee income taxes from the payslips. By changing the tax treaty parameters with its European neighbours and with a select number of other trading partners (including the United States) Switzerland has come a long way in a short period of time. The US and the EU member states will have to accept the new tax treaties as the basis for increased cooperation in international tax cases. This has worked in 2005 when Switzerland and the European Union agreed on a new withholding tax on interest payments. Switzerland was in a protracted dispute with the EU to fend off demands for automated tax reporting across borders. In a landmark treaty Switzerland agreed to not only withhold tax on interest earned in Swiss Francs by foreign nationals but to remit 75% of the taxes withheld to the countries where the bank clients had their tax residence. This withholding tax scheme became known as a disclose-or-pay mechanism designed to minimize the impact that tax evasion had on the revenue base of the home countries of evading clients. Foreign bank clients have long been subject to withholding tax on interest payments by Swiss banks. If they wanted to get reimbursed for the tax that was withheld they had to report the income in their tax returns. What was new in the agreement struck between the EU and Switzerland was that the majority of tax that Switzerland withheld for EU citizens was actually paid to the country of residence. Switzerland lost the revenue from withholding tax that foreign nationals failed to claim back and the treasuries of EU member states would get the lion share of tax withheld on interest their nationals earned in Swiss banks, even if the income was not included in their tax returns. As the Swiss Department of Finance reports, withholding tax imposed under the Agreement amounted to CHF 738 million in 2008 of which three quarters were paid out to EU member states. The agreement is far from perfect because it only affects payments in Swiss Francs and excludes dividends or capital gains realized on assets held with Swiss banks. However it has proven to be a highly practical solution to a cross-border problem that had become politically touchy and increasingly intolerable.

inside swiss banking

New tax treaties that Switzerland is negotiating with its major trading partners go beyond the pay-or-disclose regime that ruled the last round of negotiations. Understandably, home country governments don't just want to see tax revenue increase in the future which is exactly what the 2005 Agreement achieves. They want to be able to prosecute tax payers for tax offences committed in the past and they want to be able to do so based on information obtained from the banks that hold the assets that have been diverted from their grasp. In order to maintain due process, the rule of law across borders and full sovereignty of both nations involved, the exchange of information will have to follow a well defined protocol of mutual legal assistance. The basic principles of probable cause, presumption of innocence until proven guilty and due process protecting the rights of the affected individuals have to be observed no matter how high the priority set by many EU countries or the U.S. on getting even with serious tax offenders. "Fishing expeditions" such as the one launched by the US Department of Justice and the IRS in the now infamous "John Doe" Summons case against UBS must not be allowed to set the standard for international cooperation in tax matters. They are simply a demonstration of how the economic power that one jurisdiction is capable of exercising over another can be leveraged to force cooperation in cross-border legal disputes without regard for international protocol. The future will show whether the new tax treaties that have been negotiated by all interested parties in the aftermath of the different attacks on Switzerland during 2009 will let the treaty parties achieve their goals. The objective for the U.S. and most European nations was to establish a more expedited protocol for legal assistance in tax matters that includes cases of tax evasion. The new treaties allow for this to happen but it will take a number of cases to actually play out in order for the requesting governments to be able to assess whether the execution of the new rules by the Swiss administration meets with expectations. The burden of establishing probable cause of certain citizens committing tax offences by way of their Swiss bank relationships still rests with those who wish to access information in Switzerland. The Swiss have successfully denied foreign tax authorities automated access to bank information on their tax payers. Foreign prosecutors will still have to establish the core elements of an alleged tax offence before they get access to the bank information that provides them with the 'smoking gun'. This will continue to limit the number of cases for which the Swiss will provide assistance to situations where a delinquent tax payer gives the local prosecutors enough evidence about the existence of undeclared assets offshore. Nothing has changed in this regard but what has changed is that, under the new rules, the prosecutors in a treaty country will no longer have to

inside swiss banking

establish proof of tax fraud to get access to information. In addition, the rights of accused bank clients to ordinary defence tools in the process of legal assistance remain safeguarded. Any foreign client that is subject to transfer of their bank information under any of the tax treaties will be able to take recourse to the Swiss judicial system to defend their rights to privacy under the Swiss Bank Act. This can result in substantial delays in the transmission of information as appeals tend to pile up in the court system. Some of the treaty partners may not like the legal guarantees built into the agreements to protect the rights of citizens to due process as they slow down the execution of information requests. However, this is the price to pay for a system where the rule of law supersedes the interests of the state in a swift execution of its prosecutorial agenda.

By moving the debate over Swiss tax laws to the level of treaty negotiation the Swiss government has successfully blocked the attacks by the U.S. and Germany on its sovereignty while at the same time signalling readiness to actively cooperate in the fight against global tax crime. Demands for automated data transfers are off the table the new tax treaty framework unequivocally bans 'fishing expeditions'. The famed Swiss bank secrecy lives another day, modified only with regards to tax evasion. From a law-and-order point of view this was a small modification to be made. It only affects foreign nationals banking in Switzerland as the differentiation between tax evasion and tax fraud has only been abolished with respect to cross-border situations. The economic impact of the new tax treaty environment on Swiss banks, however, is a much bigger story. While the Swiss government has largely saved national sovereignty in tax matters, the concessions made to the international community come with a significant price tag for Swiss banks, by far the largest holders of foreign assets, globally. It is commonly estimated that one third of all offshore assets belonging to individuals around the globe are in the custody of Swiss banks. Part of these assets do not comply with home country tax laws and have found their way to Switzerland because of the reputation as a safe haven with virtually impenetrable confidentiality laws. The sheer fact that the Swiss federal government has agreed to cooperate more actively in international tax matters is reason for concern to many of the foreign clients that have assets sitting at private banks in Switzerland. Wealthy clients in Geneva, Zurich and Lugano are worried about the confidentiality of their banking relationships and some of them have trouble understanding why the Swiss government and banking industry have given in to the international pressure. Many foreign clients and their advisers see the recent events as a further example of the increasing erosion of bank secrecy in Switzerland. They are questioning the validity of keeping their assets with Swiss banks now that their sense of safety and confidentiality has

inside swiss banking

been shattered. The legal nuances of what has actually changed with regards to Swiss bank secrecy and what stays the same are mostly lost on them. When the Swiss Federal Council decided to abolish the subtle differentiation between (non criminal) tax evasion and (criminal) tax fraud with respect to cross-border banking, Ivan Pictet, senior partner at Pictet & Cie in Geneva announced publicly that in his best estimate the change in tax policy of the Swiss Confederation put close to half of the assets on custody with Geneva-based private banks at risk. This may well be an overstatement, made by one of the quintessential private bankers while still in shock over a new government policy he did not expect to materialize. The events of March 2009 will not actually mean the end of Swiss banking as we know it but there can be no doubt that the policy shift in tax matters has a tectonic quality. Swiss banks are a unique creature in the global context. In no other jurisdiction around the globe is there a larger concentration of international private clients. The vast majority of them have chosen Switzerland for its reputation as a place where confidentiality is sacred and where secrets are safe. Swiss banks have lived well off the benefits that the concept of bank secrecy has awarded them. For decades, potential clients walked through their doors without much marketing effort. Swiss banks were a destination for anyone that had a need to put money in a safe place. While the change of direction in international tax matters does not per se indicate any change in Swiss bank secrecy laws, the perception in the global community is that the holes in the Swiss cheese that is bank secrecy just got bigger. Client confidentiality is no longer an absolute imperative and the Swiss government has committed to work more actively with other nations in the fight against capital flight and cross-border tax offences. There can be no doubt that, as a result, the framework for Swiss private banking has been permanently altered. Banks in Geneva and Zurich have lost part of their edge as clients no longer naturally gravitate towards them. Those among them that have relied heavily on the bank secrecy advantage handed to them courtesy of Swiss legislation in the 1930s will have to find new areas in which to set themselves apart from wealth managers in other jurisdictions. Even the larger private banks such as UBS or Credit Suisse will have to redefine their business models to adapt to the seismic changes of 2009 and find non-tax related areas of differentiation in the global marketplace. There are plenty of areas in which Swiss banks can set themselves apart from the global competition. The confidentiality culture will be one of them as it continues to play a vital role in protecting wealth from unintended disclosure. The need for confidentiality is a legitimate concern to those with significant wealth. Their wealth is much less threatened by tax authorities trying to get more than their fair share of the wallet than it is by nosy third parties trying to find out about their net worth to use it

inside swiss banking

against them in business deals or court actions. Having a confidential banker in Switzerland will continue to be of high value to clients with these kinds of concerns.

CHAPTER SEVENTEEN

Levelling the Playing Field in a Global World

Some Swiss banks are justifiably concerned about the impact that the actively cooperative stance taken by the Swiss government will have on their business. How will the new framework allow them to compete with wealth managers and banks in other jurisdictions that have not taken similar action to adapt to global taxation standards? In a sense it is a debate similar to the issues of Global Warming. When the world gathered in Kyoto to discuss what measures to take to mitigate the effects that man-made global warming has on climate change, the dispute was not so much about whether greenhouse gas emissions were in fact a problem. The real issue was that some of the worst polluters were more interested in sustaining economic growth than sustaining the planet's viability. As long as China and India were not signing on to the Kyoto protocol neither were the United States or Canada. The leaders in economic power were not going to allow the emerging economies in the "BRIC" nations to catch up as

inside swiss banking

their industrial output continued to pollute at the highest levels while highly industrialized economies were taking noble steps to look after the environment. It may be a somewhat farfetched analogy because the phenomenon of cross-border tax evasion does not endanger the future viability of our planet. However, the basic principle of making global agendas work is the same. In order to assure cooperation of all market participants in a new framework of regulations there needs to be a level playing field. It makes no sense to single out Switzerland or Swiss banks as the main enemies in the fight against tax evasion as long as clients of Swiss banks can simply move their evaded assets to banks in a non-cooperative jurisdiction. You simply can't just shut down one or two offshore jurisdictions and leave a dozen others alone. This would create unjustified shifts in competitive advantage and achieve nothing in the global fight against flight of capital. The OECD realized this early on when it published a list of so-called un-cooperative jurisdictions which were put on black or grey lists. Jurisdictions like Switzerland, Luxembourg, Singapore, Monaco and Austria found themselves on either the grey or the black list even though most of them have long established tax treaty arrangements with other OECD nations. The issue was not the lack of tax treaties but the lack of commitment to established OECD standards which require "the full exchange of information in tax matters on request (by one of the treaty partners)... without regard to bank secrecy". As the OECD increased its pressure early 2009, all of the nations on the grey list have agreed to work with the OECD. They are in the process of integrating the OECD protocols of cooperation in new tax treaties so that they can eventually be taken off the list. On the most current version of this list, only Costa Rica, Uruguay, the Philippines and Malaysia remain earmarked as nations that have not committed to the OECD tax standard. All of the typical offshore banking jurisdictions, including the constellation of micro-jurisdictions in the Caribbean and the South Pacific have committed to full implementation over time. With this the playing field in international offshore banking is actually quite level. The risk for a Swiss bank of losing clients to one of the Channel Islands or Vanuatu is therefore more theoretical than it is an actual concern. Clients that want to hide assets really have nowhere to go other than the four remaining jurisdictions on the OECD list of non-cooperative nations. These four markets are at a significant disadvantage though when it comes to stealing worried clients from banks in Switzerland or any of the established offshore centres. Their banking infrastructure lags behind best practices, and so is their expertise in global wealth management. In addition it is probably fair to say that their legal and justice systems are not designed to attract foreign assets as they would be considered too much of a risk. The real choice that clients with a potential tax problem need to make is not so much

inside swiss banking

which jurisdiction to go to next. They need to consider what the right strategy is to come clean and may choose the voluntary disclosure process that is in place with most tax authorities in OECD member states. Some countries also offer tax amnesties from time to time. Italy has just recently done so and seen a significant inflow of assets as offshore wealth was repatriated. Bankers in Lugano and other locations in Switzerland lost these repatriated assets to banks and investment managers in Italy rather than a competing offshore location. As the trend towards reintegration of evaded assets continues, Swiss banks need to increase their efforts of going onshore with their clients. Larger institutions such as UBS and Credit Suisse have already established a large network of domestic private banking capabilities in all significant markets. They can offer essentially the same service quality, product suite and wealth management solutions in all major European centres and across North America. Smaller banks such as Julius Baer, Pictet, LODH and others will find getting into key onshore markets more difficult as it comes with prohibitive costs. Onshoring may not be an option to them due to limited capital resources that may make shrinking the business more worthwhile than aggressively building a business outside of Switzerland. For them, the road to sustaining a private banking franchise with an increasingly tax conscious client base may lead to strategic partnerships with domestic banks and wealth managers in the most important markets.

The coming decade will show how successfully Swiss private banks will navigate through the changed environment, how well they do in keeping their existing client base and getting new ones. Traditional offshore private banking has been given a good shake in 2008 and 2009 but as much as some politicians would like it, international cross-border banking is far from dead. Offshore banking may have lost the perceived advantage of offering the potential avoidance of taxes but the added confidentiality derived from the fact that certain assets are located outside of the domestic financial system remains a valid attraction to those concerned with safety. Swiss banks will have to reinvent their value proposition and focus more on delivering distinctive services and unique product solutions. This process is much more an opportunity for Swiss banks than it is a threat to their existence. Those banks that embrace the opportunity for renewal will come out of the current downdraft as invigorated and energized institutions with a clearer focus on what their core business should be. Those that resist the change coming their way or resigning in the face of adversity will disappear. Most importantly, Switzerland will lose a good number of the smaller banks and subsidiaries of larger foreign institutions that have been set up with the primary objective to take

inside swiss banking

advantage of the nimble yet important differences in the Swiss tax laws. The potential loss of these types of firms can hardly be considered a loss to the Swiss financial system. Much to the contrary will their disappearance strengthen Switzerland as one of the world's major financial centres. The many micro-banks whose raison d'être is not easily recognizable have long been a headache for FINMA. Many of them create regulatory issues that are disproportionate to their small size and they taint the financial system as a whole. As far as Swiss subsidiaries or branches of foreign banks are concerned their disappearance from the fraternity of Swiss private bankers is nothing but a logical consequence of the actions their home country governments have taken against Switzerland as a perceived tax haven. Banks headquartered in the very countries that have made it their mission in 2009 to aggressively take their fight against tax offenders to Zurich and Geneva have operated under the protection of Swiss bank secrecy for decades. Swiss branches of German, Italian or U.S. banks have helped countless clients from all over the world put money where the light of foreign tax authorities does not shine. Foreign bank branches have taken full advantage of the added safety and security associated with Switzerland to further their business with international clients. American banks have for decades availed themselves of the favourable Swiss banking laws to look after clients from Latin America while German banks operating in Zurich may well have helped clients from other EU nations evade taxes. The critical observer will have no problem detecting the hypocrisy. For these types of foreign banks to continue operating in Switzerland as if nothing happened would be pure cynicism. Some foreign banks have realized how thin the air in Zurich became for them and have started an organized retreat from Swiss-based private banking activities. No doubt that Switzerland is about to lose many of them in the aftermath of the OECD tax clean-up.

The change in the regulatory and legal environment in international tax matters will be a catalyst of change and consolidation in the Swiss private banking market. Diversified firms of critical mass with a business model that is geared towards sustainable value add will have an opportunity to accelerate growth. Smaller firms with unsustainable business models will be forced to exit the market and sell client assets. This process of consolidation not only affects Switzerland; the actions that the OECD took over the past years to bring about a globally accepted cross-border tax standard will impact all of the traditional offshore centres from Jersey to the Netherlands' Antilles, from Luxembourg to Liechtenstein and from the Cayman Islands to Vanuatu. The nature and scope of the financial services business conducted in each of these many jurisdictions varies significantly. Some of them have a broad economic base with a broad financial services system while others are singularly focused on providing offshore banking and trust services to wealthy clients. Some of these micro-jurisdictions may find it difficult to adjust to the new environment. They may eventually see the revenue streams from offshore incorporations, plain vanilla trust services and other templated offers disappear as clients shut down structures that became obsolete and new clients fail to show up. Some of the very small jurisdictions may simply not have a future in offshore finance while the core locations with established institutional financial services may be able to grow. The challenge for many offshore locations such as the Bahamas, Cayman Islands and Barbados will be to develop a much stronger capability in the investment management and banking sectors in order to provide their offshore clientele with a much broader service offering. In remote Caribbean jurisdictions this is easier said than done. Demographics are a major issue on the islands as the population in most jurisdictions is just too small to provide sufficient talent and expertise to compete in a sophisticated business like offshore banking. Banks and trust companies operating in the islands therefore rely heavily on imported human resources that usually only stay for a few years and come with the high costs of expatriate compensation packages. Capacity becomes an issue in many of the smaller yet well established offshore jurisdictions, especially if offshore firms embark on up-scaling their business in order to sustain growth in an increasingly challenging environment. While the challenges in Switzerland are different from the ones facing the Commonwealth of the Bahamas, all of the traditional offshore centres have to deal with issues resulting from the change in the treatment of cross-border tax situations. This further levels the playing field as nobody has been given a free ride to continue on with old practices. Switzerland is one of the jurisdictions that can benefit from the new environment as its financial institutions have a broad business base that can absorb systemic shocks in the private banking segment. Swiss banks will be around when the global private banking industry resets after all the necessary changes have been made to adjust to the new global tax environment. However, survival of Switzerland as a destination for the world's wealthy families will largely depend on how its leading private banks adjust to the new paradigms after 2009.

The frantic activity that U.S. and European tax authorities have developed in their fight against Swiss supremacy in offshore banking has raised attention to confidentiality and secrecy in financial matters across the globe. We have already explored how the OECD has employed the use of black, gray and white lists to force offshore jurisdictions into compliance with a new global standard for the cross-border exchange of tax information.

inside swiss banking

With banking confidentiality on the radar screen of government agencies, public policy advocates and media orgnizations, it is hardly a surprise that non-government organizations latched on to the subject, propelling their own agendas. One of them is the London-based Tax Justice Network (TJN), an organization promoting transparency in taxation matters and awareness of the negative effects that tax avoidance has on global development. On November 1st, 2009, the TJN released its "Financial Secrecy Index" listing jurisdictions globally according to the rating they received in a dozen categories relating to transparency and disclosure requirements governing financial affairs. One would expect to find Switzerland and Luxembourg in the Top Ten of this index and so, it is hardly a surprise that Luxembourg came in second, followed by Switzerland taking Bronze. The big suprise in the index is the Gold Medalist in this involuntary contest. The top of the podium was not awarded to one of the usual suspects, such as the Cayman Islands or one of the Channel Islands; it went to the U.S. State of Delaware, home of Vice-President Joe Biden and thousands of registered corporations. America can't be happy as its leading institutions, including the U.S. Senate and the Department of Justice carefully calibrated their focus on Switzerland and Liechtenstein in an effort to single out these two European nations in the fight against capital flight and tax evasion. However, given the methodology used by the TJN, the ranking of Delaware as the global leader in financial secrecy is hard to be argued with. Delaware corporations can be used to hold assets in the United States with an effective zero tax rate, as long as the majority of directors are non-U.S. persons. This makes Delaware a de-facto tax haven on U.S. soil. But more importantly, the tiny state on the Eastern Seabord allows the incorporation of legal entities with significantly less information than what is generally accepted practice under the FATF rules. The lax rules for registering a limited liability company (LLC) allow legal entities to operate in the State without disclosure of their actual owners. The combination of the lack of disclosure requirements with the tax loophole has attracted thousands of American and internationally owned corporations to Wilmington, just a short drive from the headquarters of the U.S. Department of Justice and the Internal Revenue Service on Pennsylvania Avenue. Controlling shareholders of Delaware corporations can hide in plain sight, availing themselves of the United States legal system with impunity. This is relevant not only in tax matters where the existing loopholes allow for legal tax avoidance. It is disturbingly relevant in the fight against money laundering committed by organized crime and international terrorist organizations. How can the United States of America pretend to lead the fight against global money laundering and terrorist financing, how can they even remotely claim the moral high ground under the Patriot Act, if one of its Federal States' laws enable the

inside swiss banking

anonymous use of registered corporate entities? The Financial Secrecy Index flagged the ultimate hypocrisy in global finance as the United States are scrambling for explanations. Senator Levin, the combative Chair of the Senate Banking Committee investigating UBS, has long realized the capacity that Delaware has to embarrass the United States. In March of 2009 he introduced the "Incorporation Transparency and Law Enforcement Assistance Act" together with Senators Grassley and McCaskill. In this Bill, Levin and his colleagues identify the issue of the lacking requirement to disclose beneficial ownership information in the incorporation process. It attracts the abuse of U.S. registered corporations by criminals operating within and from outside the United States while E.U. countries as well as most major offshore jurisdictions require full disclosure of beneficial ownership information. Levin may have been gloating when his Committee had gotten the Swiss banking giant UBS on its knees, but he also recognizes that it is time for the United States to catch up with best practices and introduce disclosure rules within its own jurisdiction. For the righteous United States, ensuring compliance with FATF rules is essential to remaining consistent and credible in their effort to stem global tax evasion, organized crime and terrorist financing activity. Delaware has been singled in the "Financial Secrecy Index" as the most blatant case but it is not the only State within the U.S. that needs to clean up its act. Wyoming, best known for its great outdoors and Dick Cheney and Nevada, home to America's sinful playground, both have incorporation laws that seem to be stuck in the Wild West era. Like Delaware they facilitate the abuse of U.S. legal entities by individuals that want their affairs kept hidden behind a corporate veil. The Tax Justice Network may have its own agenda of branding offshore finance as the source of ongoing poverty in the developing world. This may be a somewhat simplified view of a complex topic but their latest survey of offshore finance jurisdictions is to be commended for bringing the double standard in American fingerpointing to the surface. The question has to be asked why a country so obsessed with declaring war on terror and organized crime can tolerate some of its federal states creating and maintaining a legal framework that lends itself to the very practices they are on a mission to eradicate around the globe. The United States will have to force Delaware, Wyoming and Nevada to change their rules if their leadership in all matters legal is to be taken seriousy by the rest of the world. Without such changes, there will be no level playing field in global offshore finance and while the usual offshore centres have long come clean, the U.S. will become the new target for organizations like the FATF to enforce global standards. In light of the aggressive stance that the U.S. haven taken lately against UBS and Switzerland it is hard not to see the irony.

inside swiss banking

CHAPTER EIGHTEEN

What Happened to the Swiss Brand?

The events of 2008 and 2009 have brought a lot of questions to the surface about Swiss banking and the integrity of Switzerland as a financial centre. Up until disaster struck in the U.S. in connection with the Senate hearings on offshore banking and international tax evasion, Swiss banks were an integral component of Helvetic national pride. Banks are part of the Swiss brand just like Swiss chocolate, cheese, watches and cuckoo clocks (even though these are more of a German invention). "Swiss Made" is a brand and trademark associated with quality, precision, trust, reliability, safety and high prices. Being Swiss used to give citizens the right to be proud of the largest per-capita army in the world, the International Red Cross, the Olympic movement and the most reliable airline. The trademark of "Swiss Made" formed a very specific national identity together with the pride associated with the unique military structure and Swissair. During the past 20 years some of the key components of Swiss national pride

199

have come under fire and the Swiss brand has taken a number of serious hits.

When the international debate started in the late 1990s about Switzerland's role in the Holocaust, the world (and most of the Swiss) learned from the discoveries made in the U.S. Senate hearings that the fierce Swiss Army had much less to do with Switzerland's survival outside of the Third Reich than its willingness to cooperate with the Nazis and making its banks available to facilitate financial transactions between the Axis. The image of an almost magically invincible Swiss Army had been shattered. Faced with global criticism on its cooperation with the Third Reich, Switzerland as a whole was pushed into defending her actions between Kristallnacht and V-Day and for choosing survival over heroism. A truer image of how Switzerland managed to stay out of the Second World War emerged from the discoveries made by the U.S. Senate Committee under Senator Alphonse D'Amato, the Volcker Committee and the Bergier Commission. The notion that it was Swiss military prowess and commitment to defending the nation's border that kept the Nazi's North of the Rhine River fits well with the historical myth of William Tell and the Swiss defeat of the Habsburgs in 1291. The theory was so much engrained in Swiss culture that those daring to put it in question after the German Wehrmacht surrendered to the Allied Forces were routinely treated as unpatriotic

inside swiss banking

heretics. It took fifty years and a U.S. led investigation into the role Swiss banks played during the Holocaust for the inconvenient truth to come to light. But this was just the start of an American journey. The U.S. Senate was soon going to start working on the second chapter in deconstructing the Swiss brand. The second round would focus on the other of Swiss banks' Achilles heels: cross-border tax evasion.

Swiss national pride took another hit when Swissair flight 101 tragically crashed near Peggy's Cove, Nova Scotia on September 2nd, 1998. Until then, Swissair had an immaculate record and lined up with Qantas as the most reliable airline in global skies. So it came as a surprise to the world to learn that this crash was associated with maintenance issues on the MD 11 aircraft. For the immaculate Swissair to lose an aircraft and hundreds of lives to faulty wiring in the on-board entertainment system was simply unimaginable. Peggy's Cove put an indelible dent into the stellar record and public image of Swissair as the world's safest and most prestigious carrier. Swissair never quite recovered from the incident and slid into bankruptcy in 2001. The national airline had embarked on an overly ambitious expansion strategy that tied up most of its capital. When the 9-11 attacks in New York and Arlington brought international air travel to a grinding halt, the over-extended Swissair simply did not have the financial cushion to survive. Another national icon was destroyed and Swiss national identity took further damage. Swissair was considered the ultimate blue chip on the Zurich Exchange and its shares were considered a true "Volksaktie" based on how widely distributed they were among the Swiss population. For some investors, Swissair was the only stock they ever held and in the aftermath of the grounding of its fleet in the fall of 2001 many investors lost a critical portion of their savings. Swissair's bankruptcy eventually led to the birth of Swiss International Airlines and the resurgence of the Swiss brand in the international skies. However the new born "Swiss" never got financially stable even after millions of dollars in public injections of capital and loans by the Federal and Cantonal governments. Swiss ultimately ended in the hands of German Lufthansa in 2005. A Swiss national icon in German hands is a concept that the proud Swiss continue to take issue with.

The troubles of UBS are the latest chapter in the continuous saga of a disintegrating Swiss brand. UBS and its former Chairman, Marcel Ospel were the poster children of Swiss success in an extremely competitive global marketplace. Ospel and UBS have demonstrated throughout the past decade that a Swiss financial institution can take on the hegemony of U.S. financial conglomerates. Under Ospel the bank made giant steps in the United States and solidified its global leadership position in both,

inside swiss banking

investment banking and wealth management. The success of Ospel and his executive team was intoxicating. He was named the most influential Swiss in 2006 and he was a celebrity everybody wanted to be seen with. Only in the aftermath of the subprime collapse did the world, and Switzerland, discover how much risk the bank and its executive suite had taken in their obsession to take what they thought was their rightful position on Wall Street. Ospel's high speed ride into Wall Street's hall of fame cost the world leader in wealth management the astounding amount of over forty billion dollars in losses and write downs. UBS had to ask the Swiss government for an emergency injection of six billion Swiss Francs in fresh capital. In addition, UBS's toxic US assets of some sixty billion dollars had to be transferred into a Swiss National Bank funded rescue vehicle. The bulwark of financial stability that was UBS found itself at the brink of extinction, caused by a misguided adventure into the US market and a lack of regard for risk management. Nobody expected UBS to ever get into this kind of a situation. Swiss and international clients withdrew over two-hundred billion dollars in assets from UBS in 2008 alone. The disaster of the bank's losses was further compounded by the accusations that UBS private bankers had actively conspired with US clients in their efforts to evade the long arm of the IRS. It was long known in the public that Swiss banks including UBS were used as a safe harbour by many foreign clients hiding assets from tax authorities. What was new and disturbing was the fact that it seemed as though bank executives and private bankers took an active role in assisting clients with their illegitimate, even illegal objectives. Providing clients with privacy was seen is a virtue benefiting every client that depends on the confidentiality of their financial affairs. However, bankers assisting certain clients in the performance of illegal acts were seen as an example that the bank's moral compass was out of focus and needed adjustment. The scandals surrounding UBS not only hurt the firm but the Swiss Banking brand in general. They have created an image of greed and lack of conscience that affects the Swiss banking industry as a whole, at least as it relates to their offshore business with well-to-do individuals. While UBS was singled out as the black sheep among Swiss banks in the US tax case it became clear that what the world had seen so far was but the tip of the iceberg. Undoubtedly many more of the hundreds of licensed banks in Switzerland were engaged in similarly questionable behaviour. The IRS for one made it perfectly clear after the settlement of the tax case with UBS in August of 2009 that they would now start to turn their focus on the likes of Credit Suisse, Julius Baer and any other private bank they would uncover in the context of the many voluntary disclosures made by repenting taxpayers. As it turned out, jittery clients and disgruntled employees of Swiss banks proved to be a reliable source of information

inside swiss banking

for the US Department of Justice and the IRS. As the US increased the pressure against UBS during 2008 and 2009, many US clients with a tax problem saw their escape into Swiss secrecy come to an end. Some of them would not just stop with disclosing their assets; the information they volunteered to the IRS would include the names of their bankers, tax and legal advisors, as well as detailed accounts of how their suggested corporate and trust structures could be used to deceive tax authorities. The wave of valuable information flowing into the IRS far exceeded the confines of the investigation into UBS. The information that scared tax payers volunteered in order to get favourable penalty treatment would allow the IRS to go after an increasing number of other Swiss banks. The whole offshore banking sector in Switzerland was put on high alert.

Organizations tasked with the protection of the good reputation and brand values of the Swiss banking sector have reason to be concerned with the turn of events caused by the aggressive US approach. The past global attraction of "Swiss Banking" has been the result of decades worth of building and carefully maintaining a brand that was unique in the world. Unfortunately, the misguided actions of a few individuals over a few years have severely damaged a significant portion of the goodwill that has been created over the past century. The cross-border tax woes of the Swiss private banking sector are a blatant example of the damaging effects of protracted complacency. The Board of the Swiss Bankers Association (SBA) and of FINMA will have to go into overdrive in devising a strategy to repair the image, reputation and brand of "Swiss Banking" and to restore the level of trust that banks in Switzerland have enjoyed in the past. It will not be enough to defend the banking industry against the attacks from Washington and the many OECD countries that may follow the American lead. What is required is finding arguments that can convince a widely disillusioned global marketplace to look through the short-term damage and re-associate the brand with such characteristics as legitimacy, confidentiality, security, service culture, risk management and trust.

The watch industry has demonstrated in past years that the brand values they represent can be defended and improved on in the face of attacks in the global marketplace. The industry has reinvented itself with visible innovation, paired with a smart marketing and public relations effort. Swiss watches are still the undisputed leaders of quality, desirability and style. In the luxury segment no global competitor comes close to the brand value of Rolex, Omega, Piaget or Patek Philippe, just to name a few of the leading Swiss watchmakers. However, in the early 1970s the Swiss watch industry found itself in a seemingly doomed tailspin as it lost market share in the face of increasing competition from Asia. Foreign watchmakers

inside swiss banking

discovered the cost benefits of the newly developed quartz technology. Ironically, the concept of using a quartz as the centrepiece of wristwatches was born in Swiss laboratories. However, Swiss watchmakers married to tradition and the mechanical movements that made their product so famous refused to embrace the innovation. Asian competitors filled the gap quickly and companies like Seiko and Casio flooded the market with inexpensive but accurate timepieces. Traditional Swiss watchmakers in the Jura Valley had to close shop and two thirds of the employment offered in the industry was lost. It took the marketing genius of Swatch Group to reclaim Swiss supremacy in everything watches. Swatch revolutionized the market in the 1980s with the creation of a Swiss grade watch for every budget, using quartz technology combined with funky design. Swatch became a must-have for urbanites around the globe and Swatch stores flooded thousands of malls from Europe to North America and Asia. Swatch put the "Swiss" brand back into modern watch making which benefited the whole industry, including the luxury segment represented by Rolex, Omega, etc.

The Swiss banking industry and UBS in particular will have to employ some of the strategies and tactics used by Swiss watch makers in recalibrating the core values of their operations on the Swiss brand promise. While the damage was done in a matter of months by only a few, restoring the brand will take a disproportionate amount of time and effort. Most importantly, Swiss banks, the SBA and FINMA have to realize the depth of the issue and the urgency required in responding to the criticism and the cynicism that currently dominates in the media and public policy makers worldwide. Arrogance needs to make way for humility and sincerity. Past mistakes need to be acknowledged and corrective measures plotted out to demonstrate how the recovery and revival of the Swiss banking sector will take shape. Swiss banks have experience in these kinds of situations. They were at the centre of criticism in the 1970s and 1980s when dictators from all kinds of developing countries used them to create private stashes from money they diverted from their nation's treasury for personal gain. Swiss Banks were blamed with knowingly assisting the flight of illegitimate capital from developing countries to the safe havens of Zurich's Bahnhofstrasse. There even was a vote on whether the famed Swiss bank secrecy provisions should be abolished in the face of rising evidence of Swiss banks collaborating with dictatorships from Asia to Africa and South America. When Swiss citizens went to the polls in 1984 on an initiative launched by the Social Democratic Party they overwhelmingly defeated the idea that Swiss banks should do without the protection of client confidentiality by 73% of the popular vote. The excessive abuse of the Swiss

inside swiss banking

banking system by a few foreign potentates was not enough to shake the foundation of Swiss banking secrecy.

As we have examined earlier, the SBA reacted to the Chiasso Scandal in the 1970s by establishing a Code of Due Diligence that to this day is the leading example of self-governance within the global financial industry. This same code, commonly known as the CDB can be used to make the changes required to restore the credibility and trust that have been vital elements of the Swiss financial sector's success in the past. The CDB has been a successful governance instrument over many decades and provides the necessary guidance for the Swiss banking sector to calibrate its business conduct against the moral compass established in the due diligence framework. Conspiracy with clients in acts leading to tax evasion has long been singled out as an outlawed activity that is punishable under the CDB. The SBA will have to renew its efforts to remind all of its member institutions of the relevant section in the CDB and clarify what types of actions are considered to constitute conspiracy under the terms of the code. The current interpretation of the CDB's conspiracy clause left too much of a grey area and the most recent retrenchment of the Swiss government in the area of cross-border cooperation with tax authorities calls for change in attitudes among all Swiss banks active in the cross-border wealth management business. The Swiss banking sector will no longer be able to build its future simply on the attraction of bank secrecy. The Swiss banking brand can no longer rest on the association of safety provided primarily by the secrecy provisions in the Swiss Bank Act. While the confidentiality provisions in the Bank Act remain in full force and effect, the changes made in public policy relating to international tax matters without a doubt cause a seismic paradigm shift that the banking sector as a whole needs to respond to.

The culture of client confidentiality needs to be disassociated from cross-border tax. The strong bank secrecy provision in the Swiss Bank Act protects much more than the secrets of an offshore clientele with a tax problem. They are the backbone of a confidentiality culture that is unparalleled in international banking. The legitimate benefits stemming from this culture of keeping banking relations strictly confidential are nothing else than an extension of an individual's right to privacy. For this, the Swiss need not make any excuses. The confidentiality engrained in the Swiss banking system continues to be one of its key strengths. It needs to be repositioned as a virtue rather than the liability it has recently turned into. In order to compete successfully in the context of a global marketplace, Switzerland will have to be repositioned as a financial centre known for outstanding service, leading wealth management practices and a culture that systematically protects the legitimate use of client

inside swiss banking

confidentiality. The future will show how successful Swiss banks will be in reacting to the new paradigms created in 2009. In past decades their commitment to tradition has been a hallmark of success. Now they will have to marry this commitment with a new found ability to adapt dynamically to the challenges of irreversible global integration.

Epilogue

When the Swiss Government announced the fundamental shift in its foreign tax policy in March of 2009, senior bank executives and analysts alike rushed to predict the apocalypse of Swiss private banking as we knew it. There is no doubt that the landscape of Swiss-style cross-border wealth management has changed with some level of permanence after the Swiss reluctantly adopted the OECD recommendations for the exchange of information between tax authorities. However, if you look at market performance of publicly listed Swiss banks in the second and third quarter of 2009 you will find that investors are not buying into the doomsday scenario. Credit Suisse and the plagued UBS have both doubled their market value while Julius Baer was up even more at close to 130 percent over a period of two quarters. Swiss banks' market value moved in step with their European peers Deutsche Bank, HSBC, Societe Generale and BNP and beat both their Canadian and US peers. Canadian banks' market value increase was about half of the roughly 100 percent experienced across Europe and two thirds of the performance shown by the likes of Goldman Sachs. The underperformance of Canadian banks is no surprise given the fact that they navigated through the international credit crisis with much less damage than their

inside swiss banking

European and US counterparts. They had a gentler hill to climb and the Canadian banking system today is generally seen as the leader in stability, setting the example for best in class banking regulation as the world's financial market regulators are trying to find their bearings in a new environment. Who would have thought? But let's return to Switzerland: The price that the stock markets are willing to attach to a listed stock is generally viewed as an indication of the confidence that investors have in a certain market segment or company. If this holds true in the context of the financial market recovery in the second and third quarters of 2009, then the Swiss banking sector seems to be in much better shape than originally feared. The leading Swiss banks are holding their own amongst their global competition despite the imponderable effect that the changes in cross-border tax laws may have on their future business prospects. Julius Baer beating them all with a 6 month performance that is 25 percent better than the runner up is a particularly interesting phenomenon to watch. Baer is a pure play private bank and as such more vulnerable to potential business loss due to the changes made in cross-border flows of information. Regardless of their increased exposure they have done better than their integrated peers, CS and UBS. This stellar recovery of Julius Baer on the Swiss Stock Exchange may have two main reasons: Firstly, the bank is not exposed to the volatility of capital and credit markets and the potential threat to sustainable earnings that

213

goes with it. While UBS has both de-leveraged and de-risked its investment banking activities, the firm is still heavily exposed to capital and debt market risks. Furthermore the level of retrenchment in its investment bank has put UBS at a competitive disadvantage with respect to some US peers who have picked up some of their top talent. As the balance sheet and risk appetite shrinks, so do earnings. Highly sought after bankers would rather work with a firm that takes full advantage of the opportunities that lie ahead in a recovering market. As a result the investment banking division at UBS creates a drag on valuation, a problem that Julius Baer does not have to deal with. The second observation is that by and large the investor community seems to continue to put high values on a well-oiled wealth management machine. While Swiss banks are faced with significant challenges in their wealth management and private banking divisions the market seems to believe that the steady and sustainable earnings potential of their wealth management practices remains intact. Some analysts and pundits continue to predict the demise of Swiss private banking but the markets have already moved on from this debate. The offshore tax woes with the United States and the European Union may linger for some time and slow down growth in Swiss private banks over the next few quarters. However, there seems to be no doubt in the marketplace that the leading wealth management firms in Switzerland will not only survive the

inside swiss banking

battle but come out of the restructuring of their offshore businesses with renewed strength.

The story may be different for those banks that made traditional offshore banking their main business without too much consideration of relating tax issues. As we have seen previously, the Geneva-based private banks led by the likes of Pictet, LODH and Mirabaud have openly communicated their fears that an overly accommodating change in tax policy by the Swiss Government may have an irreversibly negative impact on their firms' future. This will be even truer for the smaller banking boutiques across Switzerland and the many independent asset management firms that have established a sizeable market presence over the past decade. A number of factors will come into play as these boutiques and micro-firms navigate through the changes: In times of crises people often revert to the known and there is a flight to perceived safety and reliability. This may negatively impact on the marketing efforts that boutiques make to attract new clients and keep existing ones. Larger institutions may benefit from an increasing number of high net worth families deciding that bigger is better and that this is not the time to experiment. The irony of course lies in the fact that it was one of the very large firms that triggered much of the private banking crisis. But even so, UBS learned from its mistakes and went through a painful period of making the appropriate changes. Its size and importance to the global financial system enabled UBS to withstand a level of pressures and financial stress (albeit with the help of the Federal Government) that most other firms would not have survived. Small boutiques don't have the luxury of government support and they tend to be much more exposed to threats to their existing business models stemming either from changes in public policy or even just from a single investigation by prosecutors or regulators. As we have seen in the UBS tax case US prosecutors have started to systematically target advisors as part of their criminal investigations. Private bankers and wealth management professionals advising US clients are facing an increased risk of being criminally charged in the United States for conspiracy if they help their clients avoid disclosure. The indictment of Raoul Weil and the fugitive status that was attributed to him was an embarrassment to a firm the size of UBS but would not put the bank out of business. The situation is different in smaller firms. When the US Department of Justice indicted Hansruedi Schumacher of Neue Zuercher Bank (NZB) in August of 2009 the damage to the private wealth management division in that firm had long been done. NZB closed down its private client group months earlier when it became clear that their past business practices would create a massive issue with U.S. authorities. Schumacher was no longer associated with NZB when the indictment was executed. However, the need to keep him out of the crossfire forced

inside swiss banking

the bank to close the whole private banking operation. The case exemplifies the key person risk of smaller firms as prosecutors in the United States have taken their fight against white collar crime to a whole new level. Losing a senior executive at a small investment boutique or private bank to the crime busting zeal of an eager District Attorney in the US will put the future of the whole firm in jeopardy. More importantly, the U.S. are not only setting the bar fresh for what is acceptable banking practice; their aggressive stance is likely to inspire prosecutors and Attorneys General in Berlin, Paris, London and Rome to raise the stakes in their own jurisdictions and follow the example set in Washington. This is a new risk scenario for most firms operating in the offshore business. Private bankers and boutique principals in Zurich or Geneva will have to tread carefully when deciding how far they can go in accommodating their clients with services that go beyond the normal course of business. While in the past their main concern in making these decisions was focused more on their firm's reputation and potential regulatory challenges they now have to worry about their personal well-being. Accommodating the needs and wants of a specific client may well get them an international arrest warrant. This fundamentally changes the game for smaller firms, their owners and the advisors they employ. After all the personal, high-touch service offered by the principals and senior partners is exactly how small investment management boutiques differentiate themselves from larger institutions. The flexibility they have prided themselves on in the past has gotten much less of a marketing factor in the wake of international prosecutors taking the fight against tax offenders on a personal level. But bankers and advisors are not the only ones that have reason for concern when contemplating the increase of criminal scrutiny over their activities. Their clients will have to share the worries considering the risk that their trusted wealth management firm might be forced into liquidation as their principals and other key employees face criminal charges over acts committed in the ordinary course of business. Nobody wants to be associated with firms that are at a high risk of getting themselves into trouble. Prospective clients may take their business to larger firms that can survive the loss of a rogue banker or better yet, to banks that in the minds of the prospects have the appropriate business policies in place to avoid trouble with the law altogether.

Small firms will have to take these risks seriously and start implementing changes to their business models and advisory practices that ensure their longer-term viability in an environment of ever-tightening compliance. For some of the micro-firms this will come with significantly higher cost as they have to increase their focus on know-your-client and related due diligence processes. Those firms that use larger institutions as custodians will

inside swiss banking

have no choice. They will be forced to comply with a set of new policies implemented by their custodians to deal with heightened scrutiny of offshore business activity performed by independent advisors. Hundreds of small advisory firms have been formed over the past couple of decades controlling a significant portion of the offshore wealth managed out of Switzerland. They all operate within the custody platforms of larger institutions such as CS, UBS, Julius Baer and some of the state-controlled Cantonal Banks. While membership in an accredited self-regulatory association is mandatory for such independent micro-firms to do business, some of them have in the past adopted business practices that are at the edge of what would be permissible under established best practices. Quite a few of the principals behind the small advisory boutiques have left large financial institutions to set up independently in an effort to avoid the ever increasing scrutiny of their business conduct by ever more powerful compliance departments at the banks they used to work for. This type of freedom from the intrusive eyes of compliance officers may well be coming to an end soon as the large custodian banks will put much more effort into ensuring consistent business practices across their platform. The costs associated with the changes to the modus operandi may be prohibitive to some of these firms as it eats away at a profitability that has already been diminished as a result of the market meltdown. This creates an environment of future consolidation in which firms will merge to create new economies of scale that ensure sustainability. Geneva has seen such a merger in 2002 when financial markets went through the effects of a bursting dot.com bubble. Two of its major private banks, Lombard Odier and Darier Hentsch merged to form LODH. The merger gave them the critical mass to compete in an increasingly competitive global wealth management universe dominated by large institutions. The LODH transaction was touted as a merger among equals but there may have been a more personal angle to it as well. Benedict Hentsch, one of the main principals of Darier Hentsch, had been a Vice-Chairman of embattled Swissair when the venerable airline found itself bankrupt under a mountain of debt. Hentsch had a liability exposure to shareholders and was criminally charged (and acquitted) in connection with the Swissair case. Since Geneva banks operate as partnerships with unlimited liability of the owners, having a partner with this kind of exposure was considered bad for Darier Hentsch's reputation. The partners of Benedict severed ties to the scion of one of the founding families and paid him out. This transaction took place in the same timeframe that the LODH merger came about. Darier Hentsch knows all about the risks of one of the senior partners being exposed to criminal proceedings. Merging with Lombard Odier was a good choice for them and some of their peers may find the same solution to be an option to consider this time around.

inside swiss banking

Switzerland's open banking system has attracted a considerable number of foreign bank subsidiaries over past decades. Having a Swiss bank was seen as a 'must' by many global financial organizations. Banks headquartered in the very nations that have now declared a tax war on Switzerland have been operating subsidiaries there for many years and participated actively in the offshore game that their home country governments battle so aggressively. Most of these banks will have a policy not to do offshore business with clients from their home country but they will gladly assist the rest of the world. In doing so they usually take full advantage of the benefits offered by the Swiss financial legal and regulatory framework. Foreign bank subsidiaries are living the proverbial double standard and make handsome profits from the pricing advantage that a Swiss bank commands in the marketplace. They could do so below the radar as long as the global community left the Swiss banking system alone. Things have changed though with the increased attention that the US, EU and OECD have awarded the Swiss recently. The global fight against the abuse of offshore bank accounts to avoid taxation has shed a light on their activities as well and foreign bank subsidiaries are now under more scrutiny from their home base than ever. The German Government will risk losing credibility if it allows its banks to operate units in Zurich that assist residents of other European countries to avoid taxation. American banks operating in Switzerland have the same problem. With the US fighting a very public fight against UBS and the Swiss Government, it may no longer be opportune for American banks to try to have their cake and eat it. Over the past few months we have already seen the departure of a few foreign bank subsidiaries from the banking landscape in Zurich. Goldman Sachs has all but closed its private bank in Zurich, German Commerzbank sold its Swiss subsidiary to Bank Vontobel, a second tier Swiss wealth management firm and last but not least, Julius Baer has acquired ING's Swiss private banking unit. We are likely to see more of this in the not too distant future as global banks decide that a presence in the Swiss private banking market is no longer of strategic importance to them.

Conversely, we will be able to observe a renewed focus by some of the larger Swiss private banking institutions into domestic markets outside of Switzerland. Traditional offshore banking is due to shrink in coming years as governments across the globe are changing gears in their efforts to recuperate unpaid taxes from the wealthy. Swiss banks will have to bring their business to clients in their home jurisdictions if they want to capture the many growth opportunities in the global wealth management space. This process of increased 'onshoring' has already

inside swiss banking

started as Credit Suisse and UBS have both announced in the fall of 2009 that they were going to increase their footprint in Australia. The wealth management industry is not as crowded Down Under yet as would be the case in some of the more obvious markets in Europe. Albeit small, it may well be an attractive new frontier as a rebounding commodities cycle increases the prospects of Aussies creating wealth faster than the rest of the world over the coming decade. This makes Melbourne or Sydney a logical choice for a strategic investment as global wealth management finds its way out of the historic recession of 2007-2009. The same strategy could work in Canada as it shares Australia's economic fundamentals as one of the key resource markets. UBS is currently the only major Swiss bank with a significant onshore presence in America's northerly neighbour. Canada's proximity to the United States is generally seen as a deterrent for some Swiss banks to follow suit even though a closer review of the interdependencies between Ottawa and Washington D.C. does not support the instinctive fear of U.S. interference north of the border. As to the third main resource economy, Russia, years will likely have to pass before a Swiss bank will consider setting up an onshore presence there. Russia's domestic wealth management market is not sufficiently developed yet and there are too many question marks around its political and legal system. The systemic concerns regarding Mother Russia will continue to drive wealthy Muscovites and St. Petersburg's elites offshore and thus creating an onshore presence in Moscow is of much less strategic importance than doing the same in Melbourne or Toronto.

The coming decade will see a dynamic evolution of the Swiss banking sector. The golden years of doing business without asking too many questions under a veil of secrecy provided by Swiss banking laws are definitely a past mirage. There will be significant consolidation in the Swiss wealth management market and the leaders of the transition will emerge from this process with a business model that is stronger and more sustainable than what existed before. These are interesting times for Swiss banks. Some of them will get it right and some will not. Change will be the only constant in an ever-evolving environment of global finance. Only those banks in Switzerland that embrace the opportunities created by the momentum in changing attitudes will be able to defend and strengthen their position in the global wealth management marketplace. Considering the challenges that many of them face, it will be interesting to look back at the current landscape five or ten years from now and check in to see who survived, who merged with whom and who disappeared from the map.

inside swiss banking

For Switzerland as a country, the events of 2009 will create a transformative legacy for the staunchly independent nature of the Swiss psyche. 2009 was undoubtedly an 'annus horribilis' for UBS but for the economy as a whole it will go into the history books as the year in which some of the most definitive policy changes have been implemented. The Swiss have matured as global citizens. Its financial sector will pay a significant price and suffer short-term pain but the decisions taken by the government in Bern with regards to cooperation in international tax matters will facilitate the long-term survival of Switzerland as a leading centre for global wealth management and financial services. Switzerland is no longer singled out on an OECD list as a jurisdiction of questionable repute. The political and economic cost of the policy changes may be significant but the clean-up may come with some recognition going forward. Switzerland may well see some barriers for increased international stature come down as it voices ambition to take a more prominent role in the global community. The Swiss foreign minister has recently voiced Bern's political ambition to become a member of the G20 group of nations. This is seen by many as a demand for recognition of the significant changes that Switzerland has made in her foreign and economic policy. The fact that some of the landmark changes have been spurred by the need to surrender to the relentless pressure exercised by the United States is greeted with increased criticism from within Switzerland and outside. Switzerland is seen by some as a nation that has given up the core values of its neutrality to become a puppet of American imperialism. This may be an exaggeration but when Swiss authorities arrested internationally renowned director Roman Polanski at Zurich airport during the Zurich Film Festival in October of 2009, the critical voices touting the Swiss as acting as the long arm of the U.S. justice system were heard the loudest. Movie celebrities of all shades came to Polanski's rescue stating that Switzerland had given up Roman's civil rights in an effort to protect her own interests in the fragile tax situation with the United States. Nothing is farther from the truth and it took only a few days for the tide to turn as details about the Polish director's criminal past came to the fore. What this incident shows, however, is that Switzerland's performance in the arena of international politics will be under a microscope for quite a while.

The Swiss government will have to balance the need for increased cooperation with the United States and other G20 nations with the demonstration of the level of independence that is required to maintain political neutrality. Bern's support of a vibrant global financial sector based in Switzerland is a critical part of this balancing act.

inside swiss banking

On The Author

Beat J. Guldimann is a Swiss lawyer and has a Doctorate degree in Law from Basel University. He spent a significant portion of his career as legal counsel for Swiss Bank Corporation in Basel, Switzerland and in various senior executive roles for UBS and Canadian financial institutions in Toronto. Today, he owns Tribeca Consulting Group, a consulting practice focusing on the wealth management industry.

Beat lives outside of Toronto, Ontario in the rolling hills of King Township with his wife, three teenage children and two dogs.

Printed in Poland
by Amazon Fulfillment
Poland Sp. z o.o., Wrocław